The Definitive Guide to Apache mod_rewrite

Rich Bowen

Apress®

The Definitive Guide to Apache mod_rewrite

Copyright © 2006 by Rich Bowen

ISBN-13: 978-1-59059-561-9
ISBN-10: 1-59059-561-0

Library of Congress Cataloging-in-Publication data is available upon request.

Printed and bound in the United States of America 9 8 7 6 5 4 3 2 1

Lead Editor: Jason Gilmore
Technical Reviewer: Mads Toftum
Editorial Board: Steve Anglin, Dan Appleman, Ewan Buckingham, Gary Cornell, Tony Davis, Jason Gilmore, Jonathan Hassell, Chris Mills, Dominic Shakeshaft, Jim Sumser
Project Manager: Kylie Johnston
Copy Edit Manager: Nicole LeClerc
Copy Editor: Nicole LeClerc
Assistant Production Director: Kari Brooks-Copony
Production Editor: Lori Bring
Compositor: Linda Weidemann, Wolf Creek Press
Proofreader: Linda Seifert
Indexer: Carol Burbo
Artist: Kinetic Publishing Services, LLC
Cover Designer: Kurt Krames
Manufacturing Director: Tom Debolski

Distributed to the book trade worldwide by Springer-Verlag New York, Inc., 233 Spring Street, 6th Floor, New York, NY 10013. Phone 1-800-SPRINGER, fax 201-348-4505, e-mail orders-ny@springer-sbm.com, or visit http://www.springeronline.com.

For information on translations, please contact Apress directly at 2560 Ninth Street, Suite 219, Berkeley, CA 94710. Phone 510-549-5930, fax 510-549-5939, e-mail info@apress.com, or visit http://www.apress.com.

The source code for this book is available to readers at http://www.apress.com in the Source Code section.

*To my Jumbly girl, who always knows
how to make me smile.*

Contents at a Glance

Contents

About the Author

RICH BOWEN is a member of the Apache Software Foundation and a contributor to the Apache Web Server documentation. By day, he's a mild-mannered web guy at Asbury College, in Wilmore, Kentucky (http://www.asbury.edu), and by night, he enjoys Geocaching (http://www.geocky.org), HO-gauge model trains, and the works of Charles Dickens.

His light and inspiration comes from Sarah, who just wants her two front teeth for Christmas. You can see Rich at various conferences like ApacheCon (http://www.apachecon.com), on IRC (#apache on http://freenode.net), and on his blog at http://wooga.drbacchus.com/journal/.

Acknowledgments

After swearing that I'd never write another book, somehow Jason Gilmore talked me into doing another one. This is the last one. Really. I mean it. I can quit any time I want.

Thanks go to the folks on #apache, without whom this book would not have been possible. In particular, thanks to Mads Toftum, who tech-edited the book and pointed out when I was making things more complicated than they needed to be.

Finally, thanks go to Ralf Engelschall, who wrote mod_rewrite in the first place and opened a world of possibilities for all Apache users. Thanks, Ralf.

Introduction

mod_rewrite, frequently called the "Swiss Army Knife" of URL manipulation and "damned cool voodoo" is the blessing and bane of every Apache user. They know that it can do whatever they want, but they are not always sure how to coax it into doing so. I hope that this book can remove some of the mystery surrounding mod_rewrite and make it more science and less magic for you.

Who This Book Is For

This book is intended for anyone who has content on an Apache web server and wants to improve their users' primary interface: the URL.

How This Book Is Structured

This book is divided into 12 chapters and an appendix. The contents of each are described here:

- *Chapter 1: An Introduction to mod_rewrite*: In this chapter I introduce mod_rewrite and why you might want to use it at all. Also, we discuss the many ways in which you can avoid using it, since the real expert on mod_rewrite knows when not to use it.

- *Chapter 2: Regular Expressions*: Regular expressions are an essential skill set when dealing with mod_rewrite. In this chapter you'll learn how to craft your own RewriteRules, as well as understand those written by others.

- *Chapter 3: Installing and Configuring mod_rewrite*: In this chapter you'll learn how to install mod_rewrite.

- *Chapter 4: The RewriteRule Directive*: The RewriteRule directive is the fundamental building block of URL rewriting. You'll learn about the syntax and see several common examples of its use.

- *Chapter 5: The RewriteCond Directive*: This chapter discusses how RewriteCond allows you to make RewriteRules conditional, and thus introduces a kind of logic flow to rewriting.

- *Chapter 6: The RewriteMap Directive*: When rules become too complicated to express in your configuration file, you can call an external mechanism for the mapping. This chapter shows you how.

- *Chapter 7: Basic Rewrites*: Now that you know the building blocks, this chapter provides some more involved examples of what you can do with mod_rewrite.

- *Chapter 8: Conditional Rewrites*: This chapter provides some examples of how conditional rewrites help you solve common Apache problems.

- *Chapter 9: Access Control*: This chapter shows you how mod_rewrite can be used to restrict and control access to portions of your website.

- *Chapter 10: Virtual Hosts*: This chapter shows you how to dynamically create virtual hosts using mod_rewrite.

- *Chapter 11: Proxying*: This chapter describes how mod_rewrite can be used in conjunction with mod_proxy to map requests to back-end servers, provide load balancing, and otherwise offload requests to other servers.

- *Chapter 12: Debugging*: When the rules don't work quite the way you had in mind, turn to this chapter for some debugging tools that can assist you in tracking down exactly why.

- *Appendix: Additional Resources*: This appendix offers pointers to third-party mod_rewrite resources.

Prerequisites

This book covers Apache 1.3 as well as the 2.*x* series. However, the code examples were all tested and verified on 2.0 and 2.2 servers.

Downloading the Code

The companion website for this book is http://rewrite.drbacchus.com/, where you can see examples of mod_rewrite rule sets and contribute your own.

Contacting the Author

You can contact me via my email address, rbowen@rcbowen.com, or alternatively at rbowen@apache.org. You can find my blog at http://wooga.drbacchus.com/journal/.

■■■

## CHAPTER 1

An Introduction to mod_rewrite

mod_rewrite, frequently called the "Swiss Army Knife" of URL manipulation, is one of the most popular—and least understood—modules in the Apache Web Server's bag of tricks. In this chapter we'll discuss what it is, why it's necessary, and the basics of using it.

For many people, mod_rewrite rules, and regular expressions in general, are magical incantations that they mutter over their website to make it do wondrous things. If the results are not quite what they wanted, they'll add a pinch of this and a smidgen of that, in the hopes that doing so will nudge it in the right direction.[1]

The goal of this book is to assist you in moving to a place where crafting a rewrite rule set is a scientific process, with predictable results. You'll know what difference a particular change will make, and you'll be able to determine, by reading a rule that has been handed to you, what it will do or why it's not doing what it's supposed to do.

While many books spend the first chapter telling you lots of stuff you already know, I'll try to get past that as quickly as possible. In this chapter, we're going to discuss the basics of mod_rewrite and why you'd want to use it, as well as some of the alternatives to mod_rewrite. This latter topic can also be thought of as "when not to use mod_rewrite." Many of the issues that mod_rewrite addresses could be much better solved some other way. Thus, many of the "How do I use mod_rewrite to do X?" questions will be answered with "You *don't* use mod_rewrite to do that; you use something else."

When to Use mod_rewrite

mod_rewrite is for rewriting and redirecting URLs dynamically, using powerful pattern matching to allow for handling of very complex situations.

It becomes difficult to give a better definition than that, largely because the uses of mod_rewrite are almost as numerous as the people who use it. There are, however, a few

---

1. And with the rules that some people come up with out of this process, the real magic is that they work at all.

very common uses, and I aim to cover the majority of these in the examples in this book. The uses of mod_rewrite tend to fall into a few broad categories, as described in the following sections.

"Clean" URLs

Perhaps the most common use of mod_rewrite is to make ugly URLs more attractive. For example, it might be desirable to hide an icky URL like `http://www.example.com/cgi-bin/display.cgi?document_name=index` and instead have users go to `http://www.example.com/doc/index`. That can be accomplished very simply with a single `RewriteRule`, which will allow for an unlimited number of values to appear in place of the "index" in that URL.

The reasons someone might wish to do this vary. Mostly, it's so that the URL is easier to type, easier to remember, easier to tell someone over the phone, easier to put into print—in short, easier.

There are also people who believe that URLs that do not contain question marks, ampersands, and other "special characters" will necessarily appear higher in the rankings on search engines. This is, for the most part, completely untrue. However, a large number of firms billing themselves as "search engine optimization" companies have made large sums of money by persuading people otherwise.[2]

These types of URL rewritings will often be referred to as "clean" URLs, or perhaps as "permalinks" by various software packages. Permalinks, for example, will often remove an ID number in a URL (e.g., `http://www.drbacchus.com/wordpress/index.php?p=985`) and make it more user-friendly (e.g., `http://www.drbacchus.com/perm/rewritemap`). How one URL actually gets translated into the other one is of no concern to the end user, who only really cares that they receive the article they wanted to read.

Mass Virtual Hosting

When you have two or three virtual hosts, manually writing out a `<VirtualHost>` configuration block for each one is not a big problem. By the time you have a few hundred of them, not only does it become cumbersome to maintain the configuration for all of them, but it also makes Apache take a long time to start up, as it has to load every one of those blocks.

Many people use mod_rewrite to dynamically translate a hostname into a directory path, and are thus able to have an arbitrary number of virtual hosts with a single line in the configuration file. This imposes a number of limitations. In particular, each virtual

---

2. There are legitimate ways to make your website rank higher in search engines, and many of the search engine optimization companies are perfectly legitimate and aboveboard. Beware, however, when a firm assures you that removing a question mark from a URL will rocket you to the top of the Google listings.

host has to be identical, in terms of where its document root is located and what options are enabled. But for most ISPs, this is a reasonable limitation, since they have a standard way to set up new customers, and they want those customers to be as similar as possible in order to simplify maintenance.

Site Rearrangement

No matter how carefully you plan your website, you're going to have to redesign it some day. Part of that redesign is going to involve rearranging your directory structure. What seemed like a good idea a few years ago might turn out to be not so great today. However, you want your old URLs to keep working, because people have them bookmarked.

mod_rewrite will allow you to map your old URL structure to your new URL structure without having to have dozens of redirect statements all over the place. This assumes, of course, that both the former and new directory structures follow a certain logic, so that mapping one to the other is possible.

And whatever your physical directory structure is, you'll frequently want to have root-level URLs (such as `http://www.example.com/press` and `http://www.college.edu/events`), which in fact map to deeper levels in the physical directory structure. You can do this with a Redirect, or you can do it transparently using mod_rewrite. Which of these is "best" depends on a number of factors, many of which just boil down to preference.

Conditional Changes

Many uses of mod_rewrite are conditional. That is, I want the rewrite to happen sometimes, but not always. These can be based on the time of day, the person who is accessing the website, the user's preferred language, or any other arbitrary criterion.

mod_rewrite allows you to base your rewrite rules on any condition you want to impose or any combination of criteria.

Other Stuff

As soon as you think you've heard every possible use of mod_rewrite, someone will ask for a set of rewrite rules to do something that you've never considered. The amazing thing is that, in most of these cases, there's a way to twist mod_rewrite to do what is desired. It's hard to categorize these weird examples, but I'll try to illustrate some of them as we proceed through the book.

When Not to Use mod_rewrite

As important as knowing when and how to use mod_rewrite is having a firm grasp on what other tools Apache offers, so that you know when not to use mod_rewrite. All of mod_rewrite's amazing power comes at the cost of performance. Running regular expressions consumes time and memory, and it's ideal to avoid it if alternate approaches are available. However, even when there are one or more alternate approaches, it is seldom the case that one option is clearly the best one to use all the time. There are always a number of factors that you need to consider.

Just as there are several categories in which mod_rewrite use tends to fall, there are also several categories into which common misuse of mod_rewrite falls, as we'll cover in the following sections.

Simple Redirection

Probably the most common misuse of mod_rewrite is for simple redirection. Redirection is used when a client requests one URL, and we want to give them a different one instead. In many cases, this is a simple one-to-one mapping. That is, it could be a mapping of one URL to another URL, or perhaps one directory to another directory, and sometimes even a mapping of one virtual host to another one, or perhaps to another server entirely.

In each of these cases, the Redirect directive is sufficient. The syntax of the Redirect directive is as follows:

```
Redirect [Original] [Target]
```

where [Original] is the URL that was originally requested, and [Target] is the fully qualified URL to which you wish to redirect it. When the user requests the original URL, Apache will send a redirection message back to the browser, which will then request the new URL. The address appearing in the address bar of the user's browser will change to the new URL. This approach requires a second round-trip to the web server in order to retrieve the content.

The advantage of this approach, in addition to simplicity, is that the new corrected URL is announced to the user (who may or may not notice), but also that an automated process such as a search engine indexer will update its records to reflect the new URL and stop requesting the old one.

Several examples of the Redirect directive follow:

```
Redirect /index.cfm http://www.example.com/index.php
```

In this example, only one possible URL is redirected. That is, if someone requests http://www.example.com/index.cfm, they will be sent instead to http://www.example.com/index.php, but no other URLs will be affected.

In this next example, we've renamed our /pics/ directory to /images/ instead, and we want all requests for things in /pics/ to go to /images/ instead:

```
Redirect /pics/ http://www.example.com/images/
```

The Redirect directive is able to redirect an entire directory prefix, not just a fully qualified URI. Thus, in this example, a request for http://www.example.com/pics/camel.jpg will be redirected to http://www.example.com/images/camel.jpg as desired.

The following example is simply a special case of the previous example:

```
Redirect / http://other.example.com/
```

This is what you'd use if your website moved entirely to another website. Using this example, all URLs requested from http://www.example.com (assuming this directive appears in the configuration file for www.example.com) will be sent instead to http://other.example.com. One final special case of this follows:

```
Redirect / https://www.example.com/
```

This rule should be used with care. The goal here is to redirect all requests to http://www.example.com/, and any subcontent thereof to https://www.example.com/—that is, to require that all access to the site be via SSL. It is important to note that the directive must appear in the non-SSL virtual host for this domain. Putting it somewhere else could result in an infinite redirection loop. That is, every request would be redirected to itself, and then redirected to itself again, and so on, until the browser gets frustrated and throws an error message.

More Complicated Redirects

For more complicated redirects, the RedirectMatch directive is available. RedirectMatch is a partway[3] point between a standard Redirect and a RewriteRule. It allows you to do redirects in the normal way, but apply a regular expression to the requested URL, rather than having it be a fixed string.

RedirectMatch allows for quite complex redirections and is often a very acceptable solution to many problems for which you might be tempted to use mod_rewrite.

Several examples follow:

```
RedirectMatch (.*)\.gif http://images.example.com$1.png
```

In this example, we've taken all of our GIF files, converted them to PNG files, and moved them to another server. This RedirectMatch directive is able to use backreferences

---

3. Halfway would be a bit too far.

to retain the entire requested URI path and use that path to request the same image over on the other server.

Using `RedirectMatch` is going to be slower than using `Redirect`. However, it is marginally faster than using `RewriteRule` in the tests that I've performed.

Virtual Hosts

As mentioned earlier, mod_rewrite can be used to produce dynamic virtual hosts. But just because you can do this doesn't mean you should. You should consider using standard virtual hosts, as well as possibly using mod_vhost_alias, before using mod_rewrite.

mod_vhost_alias provides a hostname-to-directory mapping so that virtual hosts can be added without changing the configuration file. Although this approach is less flexible than using mod_rewrite, it is possible that it will be sufficient for your needs.

Other Stuff

Of course, I can't give a formula for when to use mod_rewrite and when not to. But I can tell you what you need to do when faced with a situation where mod_rewrite appears to be an option: consider first whether you're just doing a simple `Redirect` or perhaps a plain `ProxyPass`.

Removing mod_rewrite from a scenario removes complexity and thus makes things run faster. You should consider mod_rewrite as a last solution, rather than as the first tool you reach for in your toolbox.

It's also important to understand that mod_rewrite was written in 1996, when Apache was still rather limited. Ralf Engelschall wrote the module to solve problems that had no other solution. Many of the mod_rewrite tutorials that you may find online come from that era and don't take into consideration the fact that many of these problems now have easier solutions with standard Apache configuration directives that didn't exist in 1996. So, even if you encounter an example in a mod_rewrite tutorial or how-to somewhere, this doesn't necessarily mean that it's the best way to handle the problem.

Summary

mod_rewrite is one of the most powerful and least understood modules available for Apache. Understanding when not to use it is at least as important as knowing how to use it. Throughout this book, I'll show alternate ways to solve problems, when appropriate, using methods other than mod_rewrite.

In the next chapter, I'll introduce regular expressions. If you're already comfortable with regular expressions, you can safely skip Chapter 2 and go straight to Chapter 3, which details mod_write installation and configuration.

■ ■ ■

## CHAPTER 2

Regular Expressions

mod_rewrite is built on top of the Perl Compatible Regular Expression (PCRE) vocabulary, and a grasp of regular expressions is essential if you're going to get anything out of this book. It's not required that you be a regular expression (commonly referred to as *regex*) wizard, but you do need to know the vocabulary. And it's a good idea to have a handy reference to the syntax.

This chapter provides that, but it is certainly possible to find more thorough treatments of this topic. Regular expression syntax is a *big* topic, and it is thoroughly covered elsewhere. In particular, I highly recommend *Mastering Regular Expressions, Second Edition*, by Jeffrey Friedl (O'Reilly, 2002). It is the authoritative work on the topic of regular expressions, and it is well written, complete, and paced just about perfectly.

The goal of this chapter is to introduce the building blocks—the basic vocabulary—of regular expressions and then discuss some of the arcane techniques of crafting your own regular expressions, as well as reading those that others have bequeathed to you.

If you are already reasonably familiar with regex syntax, you can safely skip this chapter.

The Building Blocks

Regular expressions are a means to describe a text pattern (technically, it's any data, but we're primarily interested in text), so that you can look for that pattern in a block of data. The best way to read any regular expression is one character at a time. So you need to know what each character represents.

These are the basic building blocks that you will use when writing regular expressions. If you don't already know regex syntax, you'll want to bookmark this page, since you'll be referring to it until you become familiar with these characters. Table 2-1 is your key to turning a line of seemingly random characters into a meaningful pattern. The table is followed by further explanations and examples for each item.

Table 2-1. *Regular Expression Vocabulary*

Character	Meaning
.	Any character.
\	Escapes a character that has a special meaning. Thus, \. means a literal . character. Additionally, placing \ in front of a regular character can add a special meaning to that character. For example, \t indicates a tab character.
^	An anchor that insists the pattern start at the beginning of the string. ^A means that the string must start with A.
$	An anchor that insists the string end with the specified pattern. X$ means that the string must end with X.
+	Matches the previous construct one or more times. For example, a+ means "one or more 'a's."
*	Matches the previous construct zero or more times. This is the same as +, except that it's also acceptable if the thing wasn't there at all.
?	Matches the previous construct zero or one times. In other words, make it optional. It also makes the * and + characters "non-greedy." (See the upcoming section on * for more discussion of greedy versus non-greedy matching.)
( )	Provides grouping and capturing functions. *Grouping* means treating two or more characters as though they were a single unit. *Capturing* means remembering the thing that matched, so that we can use it again later. This is called a *backreference*.
[ ]	Called a *character class*, this matches only one of the contained characters. For example, [abc] matches a single character that is either a or b or c.
^	Negates a match within a character set. Be careful—this appears to be a contradiction, but it's not. The ^ character, unfortunately, means different things in different contexts. Thus, [^abc] matches a single character that is neither a nor b nor c.
!	Placed on the front of a regular expression, this means "NOT". That is, it negates the match, and so succeeds only if the string does not match the pattern.[1]

That's not all that there is to regular expressions, but it's a really good starting point. Each regular expression presented in this book will have an explanation of what it's doing, which will help you see in practical examples what each of the characters in Table 2-1 actually ends up meaning in the wild. And, in my experience, regular expressions are understood much more quickly via examples than via lectures.

What follows is a more detailed explanation of each of the items in Table 2-1, with examples.

---

1. This syntax is specific to mod_rewrite regular expressions and may not be consistent with regular expressions you will encounter elsewhere.

Matching Anything (.)

The . character in a regular expression matches any character. For example, consider the following pattern:

```
a.c
```

That pattern will match a string containing "a", followed by any character, followed by "c". So, that pattern will match the strings "abc", "ancient", and "warcraft", each of which contains that pattern. It does not match "tragic", however, because there are two characters between the "a" and the "c". That is, the . matches a single character only.

Escaping Characters (\)

The backslash, or escape character, either adds special meaning to a character or removes it, depending on the context. For example, you've already been told that the . character has special meaning. But if you want to match the literal . character, then you need to escape it with the backslash. So, while . means "any character," \. means a literal "." character.

Conversely, some characters gain special meaning when prefixed by a \ character. For example, while s means a literal "s" character, \s means a "whitespace" character— that is, a space or a tab.

Escaping a character gives it special meaning, known as a *metacharacter*. Other metacharacters will show up in the course of this book, such as \d (a decimal character), \w (a "word" character), and many others.

Tip The term "metacharacter" is often also applied to the characters such as . and $, which have special meanings within regular expressions.

Anchoring Text to the Start and End (^ and $)

Referred to as *anchor characters*, these ensure that a string starts with, or ends with, a particular character or sequence of characters. Since this is a very common need, these characters are included in this basic vocabulary.

Consider the following examples:

```
^/
```

This matches any string that starts with a slash.

`\.jpg$`

This pattern matches any string that ends with `.jpg`.

`^/$`

And this matches a string that starts with, and ends with, a slash. That is, it will only match a string that is a single slash, and nothing else.

Matching One or More Characters (+)

The + character allows a pattern or character to match more than once. For example, the following pattern will allow for common misspellings of the word "giraffe":

`giraf+e+`

This pattern will allow one or more "f"s, as well as one or more "e"s. So it will match "girafe", "giraffe", and "giraffee". It will also match "giraffffeeeeee".

Matching Zero or More Characters (*)

The * character allows the previous character to match zero or more times. That is to say, it's exactly the same as +, except that it also allows for the pattern to not match at all. This is often used when + was meant, which can result in some confusion when it matches an empty string. As an example, we'll use the a slight modification of the pattern used in the preceding section:

`giraf*e*`

This pattern will match the same strings listed previously ("giraffe", "girafe", and "giraffee"), but it will also match the string "giraeeeee", which contains zero "f" characters, as well as the string "gira", which contains zero "f" characters and zero "e" characters.

Most commonly, you'll see it used in conjunction with the . character, meaning "match anything." Frequently, in that case, the person using it has forgotten that regular expressions are substring matches. For example, consider this pattern:

`.*\.gif$`

The intent of that pattern is to match any string ending in `.gif`. The $ insists that it is at the end of the string, and the \ before the . makes that a literal . character rather than the wildcard . character. In this particular case, the .* was there to mean "starts with anything," but it is completely unnecessary and will only serve to consume time in the matching process.

A more useful example of the * character is one that checks for a comment line in an Apache configuration file. The first nonspace character needs to be a #, but the spaces are optional:

```
^\s*#
```

This pattern, then, matches a string that might (but doesn't have to) begin with white-space, followed by a #. This ensures that the first nonspace character of the line is a #.

Greedy Matching

In the case of both the + and * characters, matching is *greedy*. That is, the regular expression matches as much as it possibly can, meaning that if you apply the regular expression a+ to the string "aaaa", it will match the entire string and not be satisfied by just the first "a". This is particularly important when you are using the .* syntax, which can occasionally match more than you thought it would. I'll give some examples of this after we've discussed a few more metacharacters.

Making a Match Optional (?)

The ? character makes a single character match optional. This is extremely useful for common misspellings or elements that may (or may not) appear in a string. For example, you might use it in a word when you're not sure whether it's supposed to be hyphenated:

```
e-?mail
```

This pattern will match both "email" and "e-mail", so you can make everyone happy.

Additionally, the ? character turns off the "greedy" nature of the + and * characters. Thus, putting a ? after a + or * will make it match as little as it possibly can. See the earlier comments about greedy matching.

For example, if you apply the pattern c.*n to the string "canadian", the .* will match the substring "anadia". However, if you use c.*?n instead, the .* is no longer greedy and will match only the first "a".

Further examples of the greedy versus non-greedy behavior will follow once we've discussed backreferences.

Grouping and Capturing (())

Parentheses allow you to group several characters as a unit and also to capture the results of a match for later use. The ability to treat several characters as a unit is extremely useful in pattern matching. The following example is functional, but not very useful:

```
(abc)+
```

This will look for the sequence "abc" appearing one or more times, and so would match the string "abc" and the string "abcabc".

Even more useful is the "capturing" functionality of the parentheses. Once a pattern has matched, you often want to know what matched, so that you can use it later. This is usually referred to as a *backreference*.

For example, you may be looking for a `.gif` file, as in the previous example, and you really want to know what `.gif` file you matched. By capturing the filename with parentheses, you can use it later on:

```
(.*\.gif)$
```

In the event that this pattern matches, you will capture the matching value in a special variable, $1. (In some contexts, the variable may be called %1 instead.[2]) If you have more than one set of parentheses, the second one will be captured to the variable $2, the third to $3, and so on. Only values up through $9 are available, however. The reason for this is that $10 would be ambiguous. It might mean $1, followed by a literal zero (0), or it might mean $10. Rather than providing additional syntax to disambiguate this term, the designers of mod_rewrite instead chose to only provide backreferences through $9.

The exact way in which you can exploit this feature will be more obvious later, once we start looking at the `RewriteRule` directive in Chapter 3.

To return to the example, regarding greedy and non-greedy matching, consider these two patterns, once again applied to the string "canadian":

```
c(.*)n
c(.*?)n
```

The first pattern will return with a value of "anadia" in $1, while the second will return with $1 set to "a". When it is in greedy mode, the `.*` will gobble up as much as it can, only stopping when it reaches the last "n", but when in non-greedy mode, it will be satisfied with as little as possible, stopping with the first "n" it encounters.

It is instructive to acquire a tool such as Regex Coach or Rebug, mentioned at the end of the chapter, and feed them these patterns and strings, to watch them match the different parts of the string. The book *Mastering Regular Expressions* (O'Reilly, 2002) also offers a very complete treatment of backreferences, greedy matching, and what actually happens during the matching phase.

---

2. When using `RewriteRule`, the variables are prefixed with a dollar sign ($), but when using `RewriteCond`, they are prefixed with a percent sign (%). `RewriteRule` and `RewriteCond` are covered in more detail in Chapters 4 and 5, respectively.

Matching One of a Group of Characters ([ ])

A character class allows you to define a set of characters and match any one of them. There are several built-in character classes, like the \s metacharacter that you saw earlier. This allows for custom character classes. As a very simple example, consider the following:

```
[abc]
```

This character class will match the letter "a", or the letter "b", or the letter "c". For example, if we wanted to match the subset of users whose usernames started with one of those letters, we might look for the following pattern:

```
/home/([abc].*)
```

This combines several of the characters that we've worked with. It ends up matching a directory path for that subset of users, and the username ends up in the $1 variable. Well, actually, not quite, as you'll see in a minute, but almost.

The character class syntax also allows you to specify a range of characters fairly easily. For example, if you wanted to match a number between 1 and 5, you can use the character class [1-5].

Within a character class, the ^ character has special meaning, if it is the first character in the class. The character class [^abc] is the opposite of the character class [abc]. That is, it matches any character that is *not* "a", "b", or "c".

Which brings us back to the previous example, where we are attempting to match a username starting with "a", "b", or "c". The problem with the example is that the * character is greedy, meaning that it attempts to match as much as it possibly can. If we want to force it to stop matching when it reaches a slash, we need to match only "not slash" characters:

```
/home/([abc][^/]+)
```

I've replaced the .* with [^/]+, which has the effect of matching any characters up to a slash or the end of the string, whichever comes first. Also, I've used + instead of *, since one-character usernames are typically not permitted. Now, $1 will contain the username, whereas before it could possibly have contained other directory path components after the username.

Negation (!)

Finally, if you wish to negate an entire regular expression match, prefix it with !. This is not going to be consistent across all regular expression implementations, but can be used in a number of them. A very common use of this in the context of rewrite rules will be to indicate that you want a pattern to apply to all directories except for one. So, for example, if you wanted to exclude the /images directory from consideration, you would match the /images directory, but then negate the match:

```
!^/images
```

This will match any path not starting with /images. You'll see more of this kind of pattern match later in the book, especially in Chapter 11.

Regex Examples

A few examples may be instructive in your understanding of how regular expressions work. I'll start by describing a few of the cases that you may frequently encounter and suggest some alternate solutions to each.

Email Address

We'll start with a common favorite. Say you want to craft a regular expression that matches an email address.[3] The general format of an email address is "*something@something.something*". When you are crafting a regular expression from scratch, it's good to express the pattern to yourself in terms like this, because it's a good start toward writing the expression itself.

To express this email address as a regular expression, let's look at the component parts. The catchall "something" part can likely be expressed as .+. The . and @ parts are literal characters.

So, this gives us something like

```
.+@.+\..+
```

This is a good start and will match most email addresses. It will probably match all email addresses. However, it will also match a lot of stuff that isn't an email address, like "@@@.@" and "@.com". So you have to try something a little more specific.

You want to require that the "something" before the @ sign is not zero length and that contains certain types of characters. For example, it should be alphanumeric, but it may also contain certain other special characters, like dot, underscore, or dash.

Fortunately, PCRE provides us with a convenient way to say "alphanumeric characters," using a named character class. There are quite a number of these, such as

---

3. This isn't a particularly common example with respect to mod_rewrite, but with respect to regular expressions in general. In the case of mod_rewrite, email addresses are seldom part of URL rewriting.

[:alpha:] to match letters, [:digit:] to match numbers 0 through 9, and [:alnum:] to match alphanumeric characters.

Next, you want to ensure that the domain name part of the pattern is alphanumeric, too, except that the top-level domain (TLD; the last part of the domain name) must be letters. In the old days, we could have said it had to be three letters, but now there are a large number of perfectly valid domain names that don't match that requirement.

And finally, you want to allow an arbitrary number of dots in the hostname, so that "a.com" and "mail.s.ms.uky.edu" are both valid hostname portions of an email address.

So you can write the preceding description as follows:

```
^[[:alnum:].-_]+@[[:alnum:].]+\.[:alpha:]+$
```

This is far more specific and will probably ensure a valid email address. There are still probably ways for it to match something that is not an email address, but it is unlikely.

Phone Number

Next we'll consider the problem of matching a phone number. This is much harder than it would at first appear. We'll assume, for the sake of simplicity, that we're just trying to match U.S. phone numbers, which consist of ten numbers.

The phone number consists of three numbers, then three more, and then four more. These numbers may or may not be separated by a variety of things. The first three may or may not be enclosed in parentheses. So we'll try something like this:

```
\(?\d{3}\)?[-. ]?\d{3}[-. ]?\d{4}
```

This pattern will match most U.S. phone numbers, in most of the ordinary formats. The first three numbers may or may not be enclosed in parentheses, and the blocks of numbers may or may not be separated by dashes (-), dots (.), or spaces. This pattern is still far from foolproof, however, because users will come up with ways to submit data in unexpected format.

Let's go though the rule one metacharacter at a time:

The \(? metacharacter represents an optional opening parenthesis. The backslash is necessary because parentheses have special meaning, as discussed previously. We want to remove that special meaning and have a literal opening parenthesis. The question mark makes this character optional. That is, the person entering the data may or may not enclose the first three numbers within parentheses, and we want to ensure that either method is acceptable.

The \d{3} metacharacter introduces two objects that we have not seen so far. \d means a digit (d for digit). This can also be written as [:digit:], but the \d notation tends to be more common, for the simple reason that it involves less typing. The {3} following the \d indicates that we want to match the character exactly three times. That is, we require three digits in this portion of the match, or it will return a failure.

The {n} notation has two other possible syntaxes, if the number of characters is not known for certain ahead of time. These syntaxes are shown in Table 2-2.

Table 2-2. *Syntax for {n,m} Repetition*

Syntax	Meaning
{n}	Requires that the character appear exactly n times.
{n,}	Requires that the character appear at least n times, but more are permitted.
{n,m}	The character must appear at least n times, but not more than m times.
\)?	Like the opening parenthesis we started with, this is an optional closing parenthesis.
[-.]?	Another optional character, this allows, but does not require, a dash, a dot, or a space to appear between the first three numbers and the next three numbers.

The rest of the expression is exactly the same as what we have already done, except that the last block of numbers contains four numbers, rather than three.

The next step in crafting a regular expression is to think of the ways in which your pattern will break, and whether it is worth the additional work to catch these edge cases. For example, some users will enter a 1 before the entire number. Some phone numbers will have an extension number at the end. And that one hard-to-please user will insist on separating the numbers with a slash rather than one of the characters you have specified. These can probably be solved with a more complex regex, but the increased complexity comes at the price of speed, as well as a loss of readability. It took a page to explain what the current regex does, and that's at least some indication of how much time it would take you to decipher a regex when you come back to it in a few months and have forgotten what it is supposed to be doing.

Matching URIs

Finally, since this is, after all, a book about mod_rewrite, it seems reasonable to give some examples of matching URIs, as that is what you will primarily be doing for the rest of the book.

Most of the directives that we will discuss in the remainder of the book take regular expressions as one of their arguments. And, much of the time, those regular expressions will describe a URI, which is the technical term for the resource that was requested from your server. Most of the time, that means everything after the `http://www.domain.com` part of the web address.

In the sections that follow, I'll give several common examples of things that you might want to match.

Matching the Homepage

Frequently, people will want to match the homepage of the website. Typically, that means that the requested URI is either nothing at all, or is /, or is some index page such as `/index.html` or `/index.php`. The case where it is nothing at all would be when the requested address was `http://www.example.com` with no trailing slash.

First, let's consider the case where the user requests either `http://www.example.com` or `http://www.example.com/` (i.e., a URI with or without the trailing slash, but with no file requested). In other words, we want to match an optional slash.

As you probably remember from earlier, you use the ? character to make a match optional. Thus, we have the following:

`^/?$`

This matches a string that starts with and ends with an optional slash. Or, stated differently, it matches either something that starts ends with a slash or something that starts and ends with nothing.

Next, I'll introduce the additional complexity of the filename. That is, any of the following four strings should be matched:

- The empty string (The user requested `http://www.example.com` with no trailing slash.)

- / (The user requested `http://www.example.com/` with a trailing slash.)

- `/index.html`

- `/index.php`

We'll build on the regex that we had last time, and get the following:

`^/?(index.(html|php))?$`

This isn't quite right, as you'll see in a moment, but it's mostly right. It does, however, introduce a new syntax that hasn't been mentioned heretofore: the | syntax, which has the fancy name of *alternation* and means "one or the other." So (html|php) means "either 'html' or 'php'."

So, we've got a regex that means a string that starts with a slash (optional) followed by index., followed by either html or php, and that entire string (starting with index) is also optional, and then the string ends.

The one problem with this regex is that it also matches the strings index.php and index.html, without a leading slash. While, strictly speaking, this is incorrect, in the actual context of matching a URI, it is probably not of any great concern. Although a client could in fact request one of these two values, for one thing, they are rather unlikely to do so, and for another, even if they do, it's probably OK to treat them as though they had requested a valid URI.

Matching a Directory

If you wanted to find out what directory a particular requested URI was in, or, perhaps, what keyword it started with, you need to match everything up to the first slash. This will look something like the following:

```
^/([^/]+)
```

This regex has a number of components. First, there's the standard ^/, which we'll see a lot, meaning "starts with a slash." Following that, we have the character class [^/], which will match any "not slash" character. This is followed by a +, indicating that we want one or more of them, and enclosed in parentheses so that we can have the value for later observation, in $1.

Matching a File Type

For the third example, we'll try to match everything that has a particular file extension. This, too, is a very common need. For example, we want to match everything that is an image file. The following regex will do that, for the most common image file types:

```
\.(jpg|gif|png)$
```

Later on, you'll see how to make this regex case insensitive, so that files with upper-case file extensions are also matched.

Regex Tools

If you're going to spend more than just a little time messing with regexes, you're eventually going to want a tool that helps you visualize what's going on. There are a number of them available, each of which has different strengths and weaknesses. You'll find that most of the really good tools for regular expression development come out of the Perl community, where regular expressions are particularly popular and tend to get used in almost every program.

Rebug

Rebug is written in Perl, using the Tk toolkit to provide a graphical front-end. You can obtain Rebug from `http://real.jall.org:81/perl/rebug/`, and it should run on any system with Perl and the Tk libraries installed. If you do not have Tk installed, you can run the command-line version, which is somewhat less functional.

Rebug lets you type in a regular expression and a string against which to test it, and then it will run through the matching process, showing you what matched where. If you have any parentheses, it will show you what each backreference will be set to. You can step through the matching process a character at a time, or at any speed.

The screen capture shown in Figure 2-1 shows the regular expression we developed earlier for matching phone numbers. You enter the regular expression into the top box, and the string that you want it to match in the String to Match Against box, and then run it.

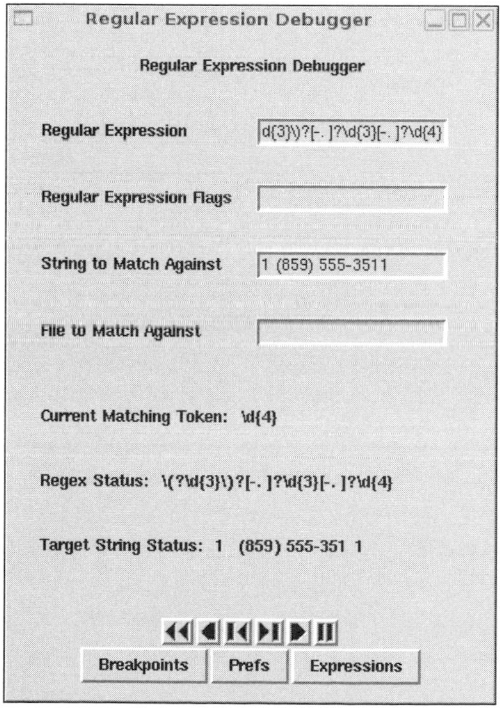

Figure 2-1. *The Rebug Regular Expression Debugger*

You can provide various flags to modify the behavior of the regular expression, but these are Perl-specific flags and don't necessarily map to anything useful in mod_rewrite. The Expressions button lets you watch the value of variables such as $1 as it runs through the regular expression.

Regex Coach

Another similar application is Regex Coach, which is available for Windows and Linux, and can be downloaded from `http://www.weitz.de/regex-coach/`. Like Rebug, Regex Coach allows you to step through a regular expression and watch what it does and does not match. This can be extremely instructive as you learn to write your own regular expressions.

Summary

Having a good grasp of regular expressions is a necessary prerequisite to working with mod_rewrite. All too often, people try to build regular expressions by the brute-force method, trying various different combinations at random until something seems to mostly work. This results in expressions that are inefficient and fragile, as well as being a great waste of time and the cause of much frustration.

Keep a bookmark in this chapter, and refer back to it when you're trying to figure out what a particular regex is doing.

Other recommended reference sources include the Perl regular expression documentation, which you can find online at `http://perldoc.perl.org/perlre.html` or by typing `perldoc perlre` at your command line, and the PCRE documentation, which you can find online at `http://pcre.org/pcre.txt`.

CHAPTER 3

■■■

Installing and Configuring mod_rewrite

As with any Apache module, there are a number of ways to install mod_rewrite. Fortunately, the vast majority of third-party distributions of Apache come with mod_rewrite installed and enabled. This is a reflection of the popularity and power of the module.

However, since mod_rewrite was added to the main Apache source distribution several years after the initial release, it is not part of what is enabled by default in an installation from source. Thus, whether you already have mod_rewrite installed and what you will need to do to get it working will vary depending on how you installed Apache.

Third-Party Distributions

A great amount of complication stems from the fact that there are dozens of different ways you might have installed Apache. Simplistically, however, you might have installed Apache from source code, downloaded from http://httpd.apache.org/, or you might have installed Apache from a binary package downloaded from http://httpd.apache.org/, or you might have installed Apache from a binary package obtained either with the operating system that you installed or from some third-party source as an add-on package for your particular operating system.

It is in this last case (i.e., third-party distribution of Apache) that causes the most frustration. The license of the Apache Software Foundation allows this sort of thing—even encourages it. But it means that those installations of Apache will differ from the documentation sufficiently to cause confusion on even the simplest task.

That doesn't mean that using third-party distributions of Apache is a bad thing;[1] it just means that these unofficial distributions make the documentation less reliable, and you may need to consult the documentation for your particular distribution.

---

1. You'll find a great deal of disagreement on this particular point, and I stubbornly (and cowardly) refuse to take a position on it in this book. Obviously, though, some third-party distributions of Apache do a better job of being "standard" and compliant with the documentation than do others.

Having said that, the following installation instructions should be correct in most situations. While some readers might find this a bit frustrating, it must be assumed that the makers of these third-party distributions thought that their decisions were the right ones for some reason, so let's give them the benefit of the doubt.

Installing mod_rewrite

Since there are a number of different ways to install Apache, and, thus, a number of different ways to install mod_rewrite, this section attempts to cover those various options. If you know how you installed Apache, you really only need to look at that particular portion of this section. If you're unsure, each subsection will try to clarify what kind of installation it is talking about.

We'll consider installing Apache from source, using both a static module build and a shared-object approach. Next, we'll discuss installing via a binary package.

This section does not constitute complete documentation of how to install the Apache web server. For that, you should consult the installation documentation at one of the URLs listed in Table 3-1.

Table 3-1. *Installation Documentation*

Version	Documentation
1.3	http://httpd.apache.org/docs/1.3/install.html
2.0	http://httpd.apache.org/docs/2.0/install.html

Static vs. Shared Objects

When installing Apache, you will need to decide whether you will compile modules statically or build them as shared objects. It's worthwhile to spend a few moments on this distinction before we delve into the various ways of installing mod_rewrite.

When a module is compiled statically, that just means the module is built into the main Apache executable file. Conversely, when a module is built as a shared object, the module is in a separate file (an .so file), which can be loaded into the Apache server when the server starts up.

In the case of statically compiled modules, you have no choice as to what modules are loaded: everything that was compiled statically will be loaded. The trade-off is that your server will run slightly faster, and there will never be any ambiguity as to what modules are or are not loaded.

In the case of modules that are built as shared objects, each one is stored in its own .so file, which must be loaded at server startup time. Most third-party binary distributions of Apache are built this way. With this kind of installation, you can pick which modules you want to have installed and leave out the ones you don't need, without having to recompile Apache. This is handled by directives in your configuration file.

Of the two options, building modules as shared objects is far more common, due to the convenience of adding and removing modules at will. It also makes it far easier to add third-party modules to the server later on.

The loading of shared object modules is handled by mod_so. It is thus recommended that you always install mod_so on your server, just in case you need it.

Installing from Source: Static

If you perform a default installation of Apache and accept the default selection of modules, mod_rewrite will not be installed. Thus, if you want to have mod_rewrite installed as a statically compiled module, you'll need to add an additional flag at build time.

If you are installing Apache 1.3, this flag will look like this: `--enable-module=rewrite`. So, when you configure your Apache installation, the configure command might look something like the following:

```
./configure --prefix=/usr/local/apache --enable-module=rewrite [other options]
```

This will add the mod_rewrite module to the list of those being installed already, and it will (when you type `make` and `make install`) build the module into the httpd binary executable file.

If you are installing Apache 2.0, the flag will look instead like this: `--enable-rewrite`. In this case, the configure like will look as follows:

```
./configure --prefix=/usr/local/apache2 --enable-rewrite [other options]
```

In either case (1.3 or 2.0), you can include other command-line arguments as well, in order to build Apache exactly as you need it. You can find out more about the available configuration command-line options by typing

```
./configure --help
```

After running `./configure` with these options, you will need to `make` and `make install` to get Apache installed and ready to run. Once again, you may need to consult the installation documentation referenced in Table 3-1.

Installing from Source: Shared

If you wish to install mod_rewrite as a shared object, either because you've already built Apache and don't wish to have to rebuild it, or because you just happen to like running your modules as shared objects, this section is for you.

You can install a module as a shared object either at the time that you build Apache or after the fact. The effect is the same: you end up with a file called mod_rewrite.so in your modules directory, in the case of Apache 2.x, or in your libexec directory, in the case of Apache 1.3.

This module can be loaded as necessary using the LoadModule directive in your Apache configuration file. This allows you to decide whether you want to load the module, and you can also change your mind as often as you want, without having to recompile anything. Modules can be compiled as shared objects during the initial installation of Apache, using the techniques outlined in the sections that follow.

Installing mod_rewrite As a Shared Object on Apache 1.3

For Apache 1.3, the syntax is --enable-shared=rewrite in the ./configure command line, like this:

```
./configure --prefix=/usr/local/apache --enable-shared=rewrite [other options]
```

This will automatically include mod_so into the configuration and configure mod_rewrite to be compiled as a shared object. It will also add the necessary AddModule and LoadModule directives to the default configuration file, so that the module will get loaded when the server starts up.

The following directives will appear for mod_rewrite:

```
LoadModule rewrite_module      libexec/mod_rewrite.so
AddModule mod_rewrite.c
```

Note that you can also tell the configure script to build everything as a shared object, thus eliminating the inevitable confusion when some modules are shared and others are not:

```
./configure --prefix=/usr/local/apache --enable-module=most --enable-shared=max
```

On the other hand, if you already have Apache 1.3 installed and only want to add mod_rewrite to it as a shared object without recompiling Apache from scratch, you can do so with the utility called apxs, which comes with Apache.

First, you will need to locate the source code of mod_rewrite itself. You can find it in the downloaded Apache source code, in the src/modules/standard directory. Change into that directory, and type

```
/usr/local/apache/bin/apxs -cia mod_rewrite.c
```

This will build the mod_rewrite.so shared object file, copy it into your Apache modules directory, and append the necessary configuration directives to your Apache configuration file.

Note that if you installed Apache in some location other than /usr/local/apache, apxs will be located at a different path.

Installing mod_rewrite As a Shared Object on Apache 2.*x*

For Apache 2.*x*, since the configure script is entirely different, so too are the options for building mod_rewrite as a shared object. To build an individual module (such as mod_rewrite) as a shared object, you may use the --enable-mods-shared argument:

```
./configure --prefix=/usr/local/apache --enable-mods-shared='rewrite'
```

Several modules can be configured as shared objects by making this a space-separated list:

```
./configure --prefix=/usr/local/apache --enable-mods-shared='rewrite dav dav-fs'
```

And, as with Apache 1.3, you can simply specify that all of the modules should be built as shared objects by specifying the following:

```
./configure --prefix=/usr/local/apache --enable-mods-shared=most
```

In this case, only one line will be added to your configuration file to load mod_rewrite:

```
LoadModule rewrite_module modules/mod_rewrite.so
```

If you already have Apache 2.*x* installed, you can add mod_rewrite, or any other module, as a shared object using the apxs utility that comes with Apache.

The mod_rewrite source is located in the modules/mappers subdirectory of your Apache 2.0 source code directory. Change into that directory and type the following:

```
/usr/local/apache2/bin/apxs -cia mod_rewrite.c
```

This will build the mod_rewrite shared object file, copy it into your Apache modules directory, and modify your configuration file to load mod_rewrite on its next restart.

If you installed Apache in some location other than /usr/local/apache2, then apxs will be located in that different path.

Enabling mod_rewrite: Binary Installation

If you didn't install Apache from source, then you've probably installed a binary distribution, which you obtained either from the binaries/ directory on the Apache distribution site or from your operating system vendor. For example, you may have installed an RPM, or you installed via the apt-get, yum, or urpmi installation manager. Alternatively, if you are running Apache on Windows, you may have download a binary installation package either from the http://apache.org website or from any of a variety of third-party sites that offer Apache with an assortment of add-on features.

If you installed a binary distribution of Apache, or if Apache was installed by default when you installed your operating system, it is certain that the modules have been built as shared objects. This is done by default with all binary distributions of Apache, so that a single distribution may satisfy everyone's requirements. It is then up to the system administrator to determine which modules should be loaded and to modify the configuration file accordingly.

One point on which the various binary distributions differ is which modules they enable by default. It's increasingly common to enable *everything* by default and leave it up to system administrators to disable those modules they do not want. Since it seems that the majority of administrators are unaware of this, many web servers are running with modules enabled that are not actually necessary.

Enabling—or disabling—an installed module in this situation is a matter of uncommenting, or commenting out, a line or two in the configuration file.

As you saw earlier, in the case of Apache 1.3, each module requires two configuration lines to enable it. You will need to locate these lines in your configuration file, and, if they are commented out (the line starts with a # character) you will need to uncomment them (remove that # character) in order to enable the module. The lines you are looking for are those listed previously, namely

```
LoadModule rewrite_module      libexec/mod_rewrite.so
AddModule mod_rewrite.c
```

Conversely, if there are any modules you don't want loaded, you should locate the directives for those modules and comment them out:

```
# LoadModule imap_module        libexec/mod_imap.so
# AddModule mod_imap.c
```

These directives will probably not appear together, as shown here. All of the LoadModule directives will be together in a block, and all of the AddModule directives will be together in a block.

Keep in mind this isn't always the case, as makers of third-party distributions of Apache are at complete liberty to do whatever they want with their default configuration files, and some of them are quite creative. Therefore, be sure to keep an eye out for discrepancies should you be using any such distribution.

The most common deviation from this convention is to put the module load statements in a separate file, often one per module. For example, there might be a file named rewrite.conf that contains the LoadModule directive for mod_rewrite as well as other mod_rewrite-related directives. These files (or this file) will then be loaded via an Include directive, such as

```
Include modules.d
```

or perhaps

```
Include rewrite.conf
```

In the case of Apache 2.*x*, you will need only the LoadModule directive, which should look like this:

```
LoadModule rewrite_module modules/mod_rewrite.so
```

In the event that you can't find any of these files or directives, you might want to learn to use the command-line utility grep, which is a powerful search tool. If you change into the directory where your configuration files are located and type the following, you'll learn which files contain the directives you're looking for:

```
grep -ri loadmodule *
```

This command will search through all the files in that directory and in subdirectories for any occurrences of the loadmodule directive. The -r command-line option tells it to recurse through subdirectories. The -i option tells it to search in a case-insensitive manner—that is, to find occurrences whether they are upper- or lowercase. And the * tells it to look in all files. If you are running Apache on Windows, you will need to use the Windows search tool to perform this function.

Testing Whether mod_rewrite Is Correctly Installed

While there are a variety of ways to test if mod_rewrite is correctly installed, we'll opt for the simplest one right now. In your Apache configuration file, add this one line:

```
RewriteEngine On
```

Then run the configuration test argument to apachectl:

```
apachectl configtest
```

If Apache does not return an error message, then mod_rewrite is installed correctly.

If mod_rewrite is not correctly installed, you will receive an error message that looks like the following:

```
Syntax error on line 265 of /usr/local/apache/conf/httpd.conf:
Invalid command 'RewriteEngine', perhaps misspelled or defined by a module not
included in the server configuration
```

In that event, you should go back and read the preceding sections again to see which bit you missed.

If You're Not the System Administrator

Many of you have likely found much of this discussion to be rather frustrating, because you're not the system administrator on your server. For example, you may have hosted web space at some website provider, and you don't have access to make the kinds of changes and configurations we've been discussing.

In your case, mod_rewrite is either installed or it's not, and there isn't much you can do about it, other than ask your sysadmin nicely and hope that they're having a good day.

Let's start by checking to see if .htaccess files are enabled on your server. You probably already know whether or not they are and can skip to the next bit. But if you're unsure, then follow these steps.

First, create a test directory in which you can safely experiment without breaking any of the content you're already serving from your website. In that directory, create two files. The first one, which you'll name index.html, will contain nothing more than some sample content, such as, perhaps, the word "Hello". Assuming you created this test directory at the root level of your website, you should now be able to load that file in your browser with the URL http://your.server.com/test/index.html.

Next, you'll create a file in that directory called .htaccess that contains the following line:

```
InvalidDirective Here
```

Return to your browser and reload the URL you were looking at a moment ago. One of two things will happen. Hopefully, you'll get an "Internal Server Error" page, which will indicate that Apache did indeed parse the .htaccess file and didn't understand what it found there because it was an invalid directive.

If, on the other hand, the index.html file loads without any error message, this is an indication that Apache is entirely ignoring your .htaccess file, and you'll need to contact your sysadmin to ask them to enable .htaccess files. Hopefully, they know how to do this, but, if they do not, you should refer them to the .htaccess tutorial, which can be found at http://httpd.apache.org/docs/2.0/howto/htaccess.html.

Next, we'll check to see if mod_rewrite is in fact installed. Remove the InvalidDirective line from your .htaccess file and replace it with this line:

```
RewriteEngine On
```

Once again, you'll see one of two things. Either the page will load without a problem, which indicates that mod_rewrite is installed, or you'll receive the "Internal Server Error" page again.

If you do receive the error message, it can, in fact, mean one of two things: it might mean that mod_rewrite is not installed, or it might mean that mod_rewrite is installed, but the server is configured in such a way as to not permit you to use it. If you have access to your error log, check for the following error message:

```
RewriteEngine not allowed here
```

This message indicates that mod_rewrite is installed, but your server administrator has not set the AllowOverride directive to a level sufficient to allow you to use it. In particular, AllowOverride needs to be set to FileInfo (or to All) in order to permit the use of mod_rewrite directives.

Alternatively, you may see the following error message:

```
Invalid command 'RewriteEngine', perhaps misspelled or defined by a module
not included in the server configuration
```

This message indicates that mod_rewrite is not even installed.

In either case, you will need to contact your system administrator, explain to them what you did and what error message you received, and ask if they might configure the server correctly so that you can use mod_rewrite directives.

Enabling the RewriteLog

We're going to talk more about the rewrite log in Chapter 12, but it's important that you're at least aware of it at this point. This will help you to troubleshoot your own mistakes as you go along (if you're at a more advanced level).

To turn on the rewrite log, you need to add the following two directives to your main server configuration file. These cannot be set in an .htaccess file.

```
RewriteLog /var/log/rewrite.log
RewriteLogLevel 9
```

The location you select for your rewrite log should probably be where your other logs are located, although it can be just about anywhere. And you should be aware that having the `RewriteLog` enabled causes a pretty significant performance drain, as well as creating enormous log files in a very short time period. Thus, you should enable this feature only for testing and debugging, rather than having it enabled on your production server.

■**Note** In Chapter 12, we'll discuss in greater detail what you'll see in the rewrite log and how to decipher it.

Summary

Hopefully, you now have mod_rewrite installed and you're ready to start using it. In the course of the next few chapters, I'm going to introduce the various directives and instruct you in their use. It is therefore important, as we move forward, that you actually have mod_rewrite installed and operational, since there will be hands-on examples you'll want to try.

CHAPTER 4

■ ■ ■

The RewriteRule Directive

The RewriteRule directive is the main workhorse of mod_rewrite, and you'll need to become very familiar with what it can do and how to use it in your quest to become a mod_rewrite guru.

This chapter introduces the directive with a few simple examples. Then I'll discuss in more detail all of the available options and illustrate these with less simple—and hopefully more useful—examples. However, some of the most complex examples will have to wait until later, once you've been introduced to the RewriteCond directive as well as a few others.

Later in the book, more examples are presented in a cookbook style, where common (and not-so-common) problems are described and a "recipe" is provided to solve the problem.

Introducing RewriteRule

The RewriteRule directive, simply stated, lets you rewrite a requested URI into some other URI. This is accomplished by applying a regular expression to the requested URI and, if it matches a particular pattern, rewriting it to something else.

The motivation for this can be anything at all, from simple redirects to extremely complex modifications of URLs for web applications, virtual hosts, proxying, or just about anything else that occurs to you.

Although Apache provides a big bag of tricks for the purpose of mapping URIs to content, such as Alias, Redirect, and Location, and their counterparts AliasMatch, RedirectMatch, and LocationMatch, there are times when none of these really does quite what you had in mind. This is when RewriteRule might be the right solution.

RewriteRule Syntax

The RewriteRule directive has the following syntax:

```
RewriteRule pattern target_url [flag,flag,flag,…]
```

The pattern is a regular expression to be applied to the requested URI. If the regular expression matches, then the requested URI will be rewritten to the target_url. Finally, the behavior of the rewrite rule can be modified based on what flags, if any, are listed at the end of the rule. Before diving into additional details regarding the pattern, it seems prudent to talk a bit more about how the location of each RewriteRule directive can affect its behavior.

RewriteRule Context

RewriteRule can affect Apache's behavior from a variety of locations, and its location influences the directive's context. Specifically, it can appear in your httpd.conf or other main Apache configuration file, in an .htaccess file, or in a <Directory> block within your configuration file.

In the latter two cases, which we'll call *per-directory (per-dir) context*, in order to be consistent with what you'll see in the rewrite log later on, the rules change slightly, but in a very predictable manner. This change tends to cause a great deal of confusion to many beginners, because rules that beginners expect to work, don't. Once you understand what the pattern is, it should make more sense why the rules don't work.

Main Server Configuration File

We're going to start with rules within the global scope of your Apache configuration file or within a <VirtualHost> container. In these contexts, the rewrite pattern is applied to the value of the REQUEST_URI. The REQUEST_URI can be thought of as the URL that the user sees in the address bar of their browser, minus the http:// portion and the hostname, and any QUERY_STRING that was appended to the URL. A QUERY_STRING is anything appearing after a question mark at the end of the URL. To further clarify, consider the examples in Table 4-1.

Table 4-1. *URLs and RewriteRule's Corresponding Interpretation*

User Sees	RewriteRule Sees
http://example.com/one/two/three	/one/two/three
http://example.com/one?two=three	/one
http://example.com/index.php/one/two	/index.php/one/two

While the first two examples should be relatively straightforward, the third example does warrant some special mention. The /one/two that appears after index.php is called the *path information*. Under normal circumstances, this information is provided to the index.php file (or perhaps to a CGI program) in the environment variable PATH_INFO. In Apache 1.3, this happens by default, but in Apache 2.0 and later, you will need to set the AcceptPathInfo configuration directive to On.

Per-Dir Context

Within a per-dir context, this behavior changes. Once again, a per-dir context is defined as being within an .htaccess file or within a <Directory> block. Since we already know that we are restricted to a particular directory, we can ignore that directory in the rewrite rule. Stated differently, this means that all RewriteRules within a per-dir scope are assumed to be relative to that particular directory.

RewriteBase

There are times when you want to subtly alter that behavior, and that's when the RewriteBase directive becomes useful. In particular, you'll want to alter the implied base path when the URL path is different from the actual physical file path used to reach your content. For example, if an Alias is used, these two will be different, and RewriteBase must be used to tell mod_rewrite about this difference. For example, if you want to put an .htaccess file in a directory, /www/docs/eg, which is reached the Alias /examples, you need to tell Apache about this difference. So, your .htaccess file might look like this:

```
# .htaccess file in /www/docs/eg where the main configuration contains
# Alias /examples /www/docs/eg

RewriteEngine On

# Tell mod_rewrite we were reached via /examples and not via the path
# /www/docs/eg
RewriteBase /examples

# And whatever rewrite rules you might have
RewriteRule ^oldfile\.html newfile.html
```

You will need to use RewriteBase in per-dir contexts where the directory was reached via an Alias, or where it becomes evident that mod_rewrite is confused as to which path to use in the rewriting.

When Not to Use Per-Dir Contexts

Per-dir contexts should be avoided, when possible, for two simple reasons: performance and complexity.

The use of .htaccess files results in significant performance degradation, regardless of the contents of these files. This effect is magnified when using mod_rewrite. The reason for this is that .htaccess files are read and parsed with every request. Not only does this generate additional file system access, but also, in the case of mod_rewrite, it means that the regular expressions used in the rewrite rules must be interpreted and parsed afresh with each request to the directory scope in question. Putting configuration directives in the main server configuration file allows for the directives to be read and parsed a single time and the configuration tree stored in memory for rapid access.

The additional complexity comes primarily from the fact that most of the examples in the documentation and in tutorials tend to be geared to rewrite rules that are not placed in per-dir scope, but are in the main configuration file. This results in the need to retrofit rules for the per-dir context. This additionally means that the same rule may look quite different depending on which directory scope it is placed in.

Having said that, it is perfectly well understood that sometimes there is no option, and an .htaccess file or <Directory> block must be used.

Per-Dir Examples

In the following examples, I'll attempt to be as specific as I possibly can, so that it is abundantly clear what is going on.

First, consider the case of an .htaccess file, which in today's web hosting environment seems to be the most common scenario for managing rewrite rules. In this example, the web server's DocumentRoot is set to /usr/local/apache/htdocs and an .htaccess file resides in the directory /usr/local/apache/htdocs/example/. With that in mind, consider the examples found in Table 4-2.

Table 4-2. *Correlation Between the URI and What RewriteRule Has to Work With*

User Sees	RewriteRule in .htaccess File Looks At
http://example.com/one	Does not see this request, because it is outside of the affected directory
http://example.com/example/index.html	index.html (no leading slash)
http://example.com/example/one/two/three	one/two/three (no leading slash)
http://example.com/example/index.php?one=two	index.php (no leading slash, no QUERY_STRING)
http://example.com/example/index.php/one/two	index.php/one/two

In the examples that follow throughout the rest of the book, where appropriate I'll try to give versions of examples that will work in your main server configuration file, as well as versions that will work in an .htaccess file.[1] In that way, over time, you'll hopefully come to more clearly understand the way in which the rules differ in the per-dir context.

Finally, we'll consider the case of a <Directory> section. In the hopes of keeping this simple, you should consider RewriteRules in <Directory> sections to be treated exactly the same as having that RewriteRule in an .htaccess file in that same directory. Which is to say that Table 4-2 will be exactly the same if the RewriteRule was presented like so:

```
<Directory /usr/local/apache/htdocs/example>
    RewriteRule goes here
</Directory>
```

It's actually fairly uncommon practice to place a RewriteRule within a <Directory> block, therefore we won't return to this scenario too much throughout the book.

The Rewrite Pattern

Next, we'll consider a commonly overlooked but important question—namely, what's the rewrite pattern for?

The way that you can think of the rewrite pattern is that it is the "if" clause on the rewrite. If the URL looks like *this (the rewrite pattern)*, then do *this (the rewrite target)* to it. In other words, if the requested URL looks like the pattern, then we want to rewrite it to the target URL. Some actual examples of this will follow in the next few pages.

The rewrite pattern, as mentioned earlier, is applied just to the local URI—that is, to what the user sees in their browser address bar, minus the http:// part and the hostname.

Rewrite Target

The rewrite target—the second argument of the RewriteRule directive—determines where you want the requested URL to go instead.

■**Note** In the Apache documentation, the target is frequently called the *substitution*.

---

1. I tend to learn better by examples, and I'll make the assumption that you do, too. Most of my technical support experience is via IRC, and this assumption seems to hold up pretty well there.

In its simplest incarnations, this is just a redirect: if the URL looks like *this*, send it *here* instead. But, as you'll soon see, it quickly gets a lot more complicated than that. For our first example, however, we'll start with something that simple:

```
RewriteEngine On
RewriteRule a http://a.com/
```

■**Caution** Don't forget that you'll need to restart Apache after making a change to the configuration file.

Now, this rule is absurdly simple and not particularly useful, but it's a good starting point for our discussion. In this case, the rewrite pattern is simply a, and the target URL is http://a.com/. This rule says, "If the requested URL contains an 'a', then please redirect that request to http://a.com instead."

It is important to mention at this point that if you are using mod_rewrite for simple URL redirects, you really should take a look at the RedirectMatch directive instead, which can do these pattern-based redirects far more efficiently. In particular, the preceding rule could also be implemented as follows:

```
RedirectMatch a http://a.com/
```

However, there are sometimes very good reasons for using mod_rewrite instead, as you'll learn in the coming pages.

The rewrite target can also be—and usually is—something on the local website, rather than a fully qualified URL. However, when we get to this point, I'm reluctant to muddy the waters any more than necessary with an example that doesn't really show the whole picture. The rewrite target can, in this case, be a local URL or a file system path, and in either case, it can be either relative or absolute. These things will be easier to express once I've introduced the RewriteRule flags later in the chapter.

By default, a rewrite target that does not begin with http:// or another protocol designator is assumed to be a file system path. File paths that do not begin with a slash are interpreted as being relative to the directory in which the rewriting is taking place.

If the specified rewrite target is to be interpreted as a local URL path, additional flags are necessary in order to force that interpretation.

Finally, the rewrite target can also contain backreferences—that is, the patterns that were captured in the regular expression provided for the rewrite pattern. As you will remember from our earlier discussion on regular expressions, portions of the pattern in parentheses will be available for later use in variables such as $1 and %1. This will be illustrated in examples to follow in upcoming chapters, but here's a simple example to whet your appetite:

```
RewriteRule ^/images/(.*)\.gif$ /www/htdocs/images/$1.png
```

This example demonstrates how you might deal with a situation in which all of your site images were converted from .gif to .png format, but you wished for the old URLs for those images to still behave correctly. The rewrite target, as discussed earlier, is assumed to be a file system path. The primary purpose of this example is to illustrate how the pattern captured in the first argument (the .* appearing in parentheses) can be reused in the target as $1, so that the rule is effective for any filename.

Note Remember that ^ means "the string starts with" and $ means "the string ends with."

If the rewrite target, or substitution, is simply set to -, then no modification is made to the requested URL. While this may not seem particularly handy now, you'll see soon that this is enormously useful in certain situations.

RewriteRule Flags

In standard regular expression syntax, there are a number of flags that can be added to the end of a regex pattern. In mod_rewrite, some of these standard regular expression flags, as well as some others more specific to URL handling, may appear at the end of the rule in square brackets in order to modify the behavior of a rewrite rule:

```
RewriteRule monkey http://monkeys.com/ [R,L]
```

When no flag is provided, a default behavior will be used, depending on the nature of the arguments provided. It is my recommendation that you always use an explicit rewrite flag, so that there is never any chance of confusion, either for you or for the mod_rewrite engine.

In this section, the flags are introduced in alphabetical order, rather in any kind of logical order. So, you may want to read through the list quickly once, and then go through it again in more detail the second time, so that you know what other flags are available.

Flags can be used in either their verbose form, or in their one- or two- (and, in one case three-) letter abbreviations. It is much more common to use the abbreviation, but using the more verbose form will tend to make your rules more readable. I'll tend to use the abbreviated notation, since that is the notation that you'll encounter more often "in the wild."

Chain: C

The [chain], or [C], flag indicates that a series of rules are chained together into a single logical unit. This construct is most commonly used when a transformation is sufficiently complex that it makes sense to break it into several smaller transformations.

If a given rule succeeds, then the next rule is run as well. However, if a given rule fails, then all following rules within that chain are skipped.

Cookie: CO

Using the [cookie], or [CO], flag allows you to set a cookie as part of a rewriting transaction. You must specify three values: the name, value, and domain of the cookie. You may additionally set the duration and path of the cookie:

```
'cookie|CO=Name:Value:Domain[:Lifetime[:Path]]'
```

For example, consider the following rewrite rule:

```
RewriteRule ^/index.html - [CO=frontdoor:yes:.example.com]
```

This example will set a cookie called `frontdoor` with a value of `yes` when someone visits the URL `/index.html` on our server. This may be used to verify that someone came in through the "front door," rather than via another link.

■**Note** Remember that the - value for the substitution means that the requested URL should not be modified.

The `Lifetime` argument indicates, in minutes, how long the cookie should be retained. If this value is not set, or if it is set to `0`, the cookie will be a *session* cookie. Which is to say, it will last only for the lifetime of the browser session, and then it will be discarded.

The `Path` argument, by default, is set to `/`, meaning that the cookie will be valid for the entire site. Setting this value to something else can cause a cookie to be restricted to a smaller portion of the website.

Thus, a more complete example, containing all of the available variables, might look like the following:

```
RewriteRule ^/index.html - [cookie=frontdoor:yes:.example.com:10080:/]
```

This example will set a cookie lasting for one week (10,080 minutes is one week), and valid for any host in the `.example.com` domain.

As mentioned earlier, things are slightly different when operating out of an `.htaccess` file. Supposing the preceding rule was placed in an `.htaccess` file within the document directory containing the `index.html` file, you would need to modify it slightly, as follows:

```
RewriteRule ^index.html - [CO=frontdoor:yes:.example.com:10080:/]
```

In this case, I've used the short form (CO) rather than the long form (cookie). You should use whichever one makes the most sense to you.

Note You can read more about cookies at http://www.faqs.org/rfcs/rfc2109.html.

Env: E

The [env], or [E], flag allows you to set the value of any environment variable. This environment variable will then be available in a variety of contexts, so that it can be used in PHP code, or CGI programs, or in various configuration directives within the Apache configuration.

It is generally most useful to create your own environment variables, since using one that is already in use tends to be unreliable. In particular, the variable may be assigned its value after your rewrite rules run, undoing your hard work.

The following rather simple example sets an environment variable based on the name of the file being served. Then we use that environment variable in our logging directive to ignore certain entries in the log file:

```
RewriteEngine On
RewriteRule \.jpg$ - [env=dontlog:1]
CustomLog /var/log/apache/access_log combined env=!dontlog
```

The preceding block will set the dontlog environment variable to 1 whenever the requested URL ends in .jpg, and, in conjunction with the CustomLog directive, it will ensure that these requests don't end up getting logged.

Note As with many of the examples offered in these initial chapters, this one is a little too simplistic and can be more efficiently done a different way. In particular, instead of the RewriteRule, we could instead do the following:

```
SetEnvIf REQUEST_URI "\.jpg$" dontlog=1
```

Once you have more tools available to you, the examples will be much more useful in the real world. Since a lot of the skill involved in using mod_rewrite is in knowing when not to use it, this can be a little frustrating when you're starting up, but you'll make up for it a little later on.

You can also set several environment variables, if you like, within a comma-separated list:

```
RewriteRule \.png$ [E=image:true,E=png:true]
```

In this case, two environment variables are set. The environment variable image is set to the value true, and the environment variable png is also set to the value true.

Forbidden: F

The Forbidden, or [F], flag forces an HTTP 403 Forbidden status code. This is extremely useful, as it allows you to forbid access to various resources based on any arbitrary criterion, such as a pattern in the request, the browser type, or the time of day. The following example[2] demonstrates how to block access to a request from a machine that is infected with the Nimda IIS worm (or one of its many variants):

```
RewriteEngine On
RewriteRule (cmd|root)\.exe - [F]
```

The rewrite pattern in this example looks for a request that contains either cmd.exe or root.exe, which are two of the target URLs of that worm.

Using this technique in conjunction with the [E] flag just introduced, you could also eliminate these entries from your log files, since you already know that your Apache server is not susceptible to this worm:

```
RewriteRule (cmd|root)\.exe - [F,E=dontlog:1]
```

■Note For pattern-based URL blocking, you should also consider ModSecurity (http://www.modsecurity.org/), a very flexible "HTTP firewall" that allows for a variety of URL exclusion rules in a syntax more attuned to specifically that goal.

Gone: G

The Gone, or [G], flag causes Apache to send an HTTP 410 Gone status code, indicating that the requested URL no longer exists on the server. Among other things, this is an easy way to get search engines to remove certain URLs from their indexes:

```
RewriteRule \.cfm$ - [G]
```

---

2. Our first useful example so far!

Handler: H

The Handler, or [H], flag is new with Apache 2.2 and forces the target URL to be handled with the specified content-handler. You could, for example, force particular files to be handled by the mod_php handler:

```
RewriteRule ^/thread/(.*) /var/www/index.php?threadID=$1 ➡
[H=application/x-httpd-php]
```

This example is one of a larger class of rewrite rules, which are collectively referred to as *clean URLs* or as a variety of other similar names. The general goal of these sorts of rules is to make URLs easier to type, remember, and read. A URL that looks like http://example.com/thread/2 is much easier for the average person to remember than one that looks like http://example.com/index.php?threadID=2, and the preceding rule makes exactly that transition.

Forcing the handler type prevents the condition in which the resulting file target is served as plain text, bypassing the PHP handler. The same technique can be used for any other handler, such as the cgi-script handler.

If you are using a version of Apache earlier than 2.2, this behavior can usually be replicated using the [T] flag to set a MIME type, forcing a particular behavior. For example, whereas with 2.2 you would use [H=cgi-script] to force a particular target to be handled by mod_cgi, in earlier versions of Apache, you would instead use [T=application/x-httpd-cgi] to accomplish the same thing.

Last: L

The Last, or [l], flag indicates that the end of the rewriting process has been reached, and no further transitions should be applied to the requested URL. This is equivalent to the break or last statement in many programming languages.

This flag is only useful when several rules are chained together in a single logical unit. However, it is good form to use this flag even when just a single rule is used. This is more of a reminder for you than for mod_rewrite.

Next: N

The Next, or [N], flag can be somewhat dangerous and should not be used unless you're really sure that this is what you want to do. Use of the [N] flag indicates that the rewriting process should be started all over again from the beginning. The next run through the rewriting process is done with the rewritten URL, not the originally requested URL.

This technique is typically used in order to do a modification that appears multiple times in a URL. Thus, it is run through the rewrite process several times to ensure that all occurrences were caught.

The danger with this technique is that it is very easy to get caught in an infinite loop when using the [N] flag. In many cases, the RewriteMap directive might be a better way to handle these scenarios.

However, to offer one simple example, consider this rule, which replaces - (dash) with _ (underscore) throughout a URI:

```
RewriteRule (.*)-(.*) $1_$2 [N]
```

This rule will run repeatedly until there are no more dashes in the requested URI. For example, if a requested URI looks like /x--y-z, the rule will be run three times—once for each dash in the URI—and then exit when there are no more dashes.

No Case: NC

Adding the No Case, or [NC], flag to any RewriteRule makes that rule case insensitive. That is, a rule with this flag will not care whether the text that it is considering is uppercase or lowercase. The default behavior of the RewriteRule directive is to be case sensitive.

■**Caution** Case-insensitive pattern matching will be slightly slower.

```
RewriteRule ^/article/(\d*) /var/www/index.php?articleID=$1 \
   [NC,H=application/x-httpd-php]
```

This example will look for URLs that look like /article/12 or perhaps like /Article/173 and rewrite those URLs to be an argument to another URL—in this case, a PHP file.

No Escape: NE

If the target URL of a RewriteRule contains special characters (generally speaking, any nonalphanumeric characters), those characters will be converted into their hexcode equivalents. For example, if a target URL contains a percentage sign (%), that character will instead be converted to its equivalent representation, %25.

There are, of course, times when this is not desirable, and you do in fact want the literal character that you have specified to appear in the rewritten URL. One common example of this is the # character, which, in HTML, allows you to jump to a particular named section of a document. By default, if a # character appears in a rewrite target, it will be converted to %23, which will cause the rewritten URL to fail. By using the [NE] flag, this can be avoided:

```
RewriteRule ^/docs/(.*) /usr/docs/directives.html#$1 [NE]
```

This rule takes a request for a particular configuration directive and maps that to the exact location within a larger document listing all of the directives. And the [NE] flag ensures that the # is actually treated as an anchor.

No Subrequest: NS

The No Subrequest, or [NS], flag is extremely useful when one file includes another file via a subrequest. For example, when an HTML file includes other HTML files via the Server-Side Include (SSI) mechanism, the included files are requested from Apache via a subrequest. Generally, you don't want your RewriteRules applying to these subrequests, since that would cause the request paths to be broken. The [NS] flag specifies that the rule should not be applied to requests if they are subrequests.

Images and CSS files embedded in an HTML page are *not* retrieved via subrequests.

```
RewriteRule ^/ssi/(.*) /includes/files/$1 [NS]
```

Proxy: P

Using the Proxy, or [P], flag forces the rewritten URL to be fetched from another server via the proxy mechanism provided by mod_proxy. You must have mod_proxy installed in order to use the [P] flag. The rewrite target argument must be a fully qualified URL.

We will return to the topic of proxying in Chapter 11, and so just one example is offered here. In this example, we wish to have all images served from a dedicated image server.

```
RewriteRule ^/images/(.*) http://images.example.com/$1 [P]
ProxyPassReverse /images http://images.example.com
```

Further explanation of this example will be left until Chapter 11.

Passthru: PT

As mentioned earlier, by default, a rewrite target not starting with http:// or other protocol indicator is interpreted to mean a file path. If the path does not start with a leading slash, it is interpreted to be a file path relative to the current directory. If it does start with a slash, it is interpreted as an absolute file system path. This can be exceedingly inconvenient in many cases. Two particular cases bear describing.

The most common case is when you want to provide a URL path, and it is inconvenient to provide a full file system path.

The more serious case is when the target of a rewrite is a CGI program or other dynamic content. When a URL request is rewritten to a file path, the usual mechanisms for handling this content are bypassed, and the file is served to the client in its raw form:

```
RewriteRule ^/images/(.*)\.gif /usr/local/apache/cgi-bin/images.pl?gif=$1
```

This example, as given here, has the rather unexpected result of serving unexecuted Perl code to the browser, because it has bypassed the ScriptAlias mechanism, which relies on the URL starting with /cgi-bin/.

To get around these cases, the [PT] flag causes the rewrite target to be passed back to the URL mapping engine, so that it is treated like a URL rather than like a file path. The preceding example would become

```
RewriteRule ^/images/(.*)\.gif /cgi-bin/images.pl?gif=$1 [PT]
```

Similarly, whenever Alias is used to map a URI to a directory, it is very useful to use [PT] so that the rewrite target can use the Alias path, rather than the full directory path.

Many people, once aware of the [PT] flag, start using it all the time. It tends to be far more convenient than providing file paths, and, as a bonus, it ensures that the target is treated the way that most people *expect* it to be treated: as a URL. This flag's greater ease of use may make up for what it lacks in efficiency for many server administrators.

Query String Append: QSA

By default, the RewriteRule directive ignores QUERY_STRING arguments. To remedy this deficiency, the Query String Append, or [QSA], flag causes the QUERY_STRING to be retained exactly as it is and tacked onto the end of the resulting request, in addition to anything that may have been put there during the rewriting of the URL. The default behavior, without the [QSA] flag, is to replace the existing QUERY_STRING with the new one.

Since the use of the ordinary Redirect (and RedirectMatch) directive does not retain QUERY_STRING arguments at all, it is often useful to use the [QSA] flag in attempts to construct redirects that retain these arguments:

```
RewriteRule ^/example.php$ /cgi-bin/index.cgi [PT,QSA]
```

In this case, any QUERY_STRING arguments sent to the URL /example.php will instead be sent to /cgi-bin/index.cgi.

Redirect: R

The Redirect, or [R], flag forces an HTTP 302 Redirect to be sent to the client. This means, among other things, that the new URL will appear in the browser's address bar, whereas most of the other uses of RewriteRule leave the end user completely unaware that any rewriting occurred.

Most of the time when people use mod_rewrite to do URL redirection, the Redirect or RedirectMatch directives are actually a better choice than RewriteRule. However, there are certainly many cases when doing a redirect via RewriteRule is appropriate. In this example, a redirect is necessary so that the browser is not confused about the type of the image being served:

```
RewriteRule ^/images/(.*)\.gif /jpegs/$1.jpg [L,R]
```

You will usually want to use an [L] flag in conjunction with the [R] flag, to ensure that the redirection happens immediately and further rewriting does not occur.

■**Note** When the rewrite target is a fully qualified URL (complete with http://), redirection is the default behavior.

If you want to have a different redirection status code used, you can specify this as an argument to the [R] flag:

```
RewriteRule ^/images/(.*\.gif) /jpegs/$1.jpg [L,R=301]
```

Skip: S

The Skip, or [S], flag causes the rewrite engine to skip the next *n* rules, when the current rule matches. This may be used to build an if/else structure. The rules skipped become the *else* clause, since they are skipped when the *if* clause matches.

The motivation for this might become more apparent once the RewriteCond directive has been introduced, so explaining this flag will require a bit of a preview. RewriteCond allows you to apply a condition to the running of a RewriteRule. However, the RewriteCond directive only applies to one following RewriteRule. To force it to apply to multiple RewriteRule directives, you could use the [S] flag.

In the example that follows, we want to run the RewriteRules only if the requested filename doesn't exist:

```
RewriteCond %{REQUEST_FILENAME} -f [OR]
RewriteCond %{REQUEST_FILENAME} -d
RewriteRule . - [S=2]
RewriteRule ^journal/(.*)$ index.php?arg=$1
RewriteRule ^feed/(.*)$ rss.php?arg=$1
```

This example causes the next two rules to be skipped if the requested URI corresponds with an actual file or directory. This can be thought of as a GOTO statement of sorts, if there are more rules following the two in the example.

Type: T

The Type, or [T], flag forces the resulting URL to be served with the content-type set to whatever is specified as the argument. The example given in the documentation causes URL requests ending in .phps to be answered by the source code of the associated PHP file, passed through the syntax highlighting functionality provided with mod_php:

```
RewriteRule ^(.+\.php)s$ $1 [T=application/x-httpd-php-source]
```

This technique can be used to force a particular document type on any requested URL.

Summary

The RewriteRule directive, as the heart and soul of mod_rewrite, has an enormous number of options and, as such, can tend to be rather confusing. Using this chapter and the mod_rewrite documentation as our reference manuals, we'll attempt throughout the rest of the book to put much of our knowledge about RewriteRule into practice, along with the various other directives which mod_rewrite offers.

CHAPTER 5

■ ■ ■

The RewriteCond Directive

When discussing the RewriteRule directive, we have already encountered several situations in which it would have been nice to be able to apply a condition on the rewrite. Indeed, several of the examples in Chapter 4 were a little hokey, specifically because we were unable to apply any conditions. By "conditions," I mean that we only want to do a particular rewrite under certain circumstances. The RewriteCond directive supplies this ability and may be used before a RewriteRule to impose such a condition on the execution of that rule.

In this chapter, I'll introduce the syntax and use of the directive, and then give a number of examples that illustrate its use.

RewriteCond Syntax

The RewriteRule directive allows you to look for patterns in the requested URL—that is, the REQUEST_URI variable. RewriteCond, on the other hand, allows you to look in any variable at all. The syntax of the directive is as follows:

```
RewriteCond TestString Pattern [Flags]
```

For example, we might wish to run a RewriteRule only if the rule has not already been performed. This is a common thing to want to do, in order to prevent a rule from looping:

```
RewriteEngine On
RewriteCond %{REQUEST_URI} !^/index.php
RewriteRule (.*) /index.php?file=$1 [PT,L]
```

The preceding rule set will tack on any URL request as an argument to index.php. However, it will only do this if the URL request doesn't already start with index.php, thus preventing an infinite loop of rewrites.

The TestString can be a literal string, or it can contain variables. It is then compared to the pattern. In the event that it matches, the rule following it is executed. If it does not match, then the rule is skipped.

The actual order of execution is the reverse of what you might expect. The RewriteCond is tried only if the RewriteRule has matched. But, conceptually, you should think of them as "If this condition is met, run this RewriteRule."

The variable contents of the TestString can be of a number of different types. You can use backreferences from the most recent RewriteRule, using the $N syntax, where N is in the range 0–9. (See Chapter 4 for more details on backreferences in RewriteRules.)

```
RewriteRule (.*) /index.php?$1 [PT]
RewriteCond $1 \.jpg$
RewriteRule . - [E=jpg:1]
```

This example, having already rewritten a URL, then additionally sets an environment variable based on the original value of the requested URL.

You can use backreferences of the form %N, which refer to patterns captured in the most recent RewriteCond directive.

```
RewriteCond %{HTTP_HOST} ^www\.^([^.]+)\.com$ [NC]
RewriteCond %1 !^example$ [NC]
RewriteRule (.*) /home/%{HTTP_HOST}$1
```

This example maps a request to a particular virtual host directory, but only if the hostname matched in the first RewriteCond doesn't happen to be example.com.

You can also use RewriteMap expansions, which will be discussed in more detail in Chapter 6.

RewriteCond Variables

Alternatively, you can use any of the available server variables shown in Table 5-1. A server variable is referenced with the syntax %{VARIABLE_NAME}.

Table 5-1. *RewriteCond Variables*

Variable Name	Description
Client Variables	
HTTP_USER_AGENT	The user's browser product information.
HTTP_ACCEPT	A list of the content types that this client is willing to accept.
REMOTE_ADDR	The IP address of the requesting client.
REMOTE_HOST	The hostname of the requesting client. In practice, this is usually the same as the REMOTE_ADDR, since most servers are configured to not do IP address lookups.
REMOTE_PORT	The client TCP port from which the connection was made.

Variable Name	Description
REMOTE_USER	In the case where access to the resource requires authentication, this variable contains the username with which the user authenticated.
REMOTE_IDENT	In practice, this is always blank. It used to contain identifying information, or the email address of the remote user.
HTTP_PROXY_CONNECTION	This variable contains the address of the proxy server, if any, through which the connection was made.
HTTP_FORWARDED	This variable may or may not contain the address of the original client address, in the event that the request was made through a proxy server.
Request Variables	
HTTP_REFERER	The website address (URL) from which the user followed a link to this location.
HTTP_COOKIE	The value of the cookie header, containing the cookies associated with the requested URL, if any.
HTTP_HOST	The hostname portion of the URL that was requested. This is the virtual host (or the server name) from which the content was requested. This is usually consulted when doing virtual host–based rewrites.
REQUEST_METHOD	The request method used, such as GET or POST.
SCRIPT_FILENAME	Contains the full file path to the script that is serving the request.
PATH_INFO	Additional data passed at the end of the URL following a slash. For example, in the URL http://www.example.con/index.php/more/data, the value of PATH_INFO is /more/data.
QUERY_STRING	Additional data passed at the end of the URL following a question mark. For example, in the URL http://www.example.com/test.pl?one=two&three=four, the value of QUERY_STRING is one=two&three=four.
AUTH_TYPE	The authentication type that was used to authenticate the user. This will usually be either BASIC or DIGEST, and it will be set only if authentication was required to reach this resource.
Server Variables	
DOCUMENT_ROOT	The value of the DocumentRoot configuration variable in the current virtual host.
SERVER_ADMIN	The email address of the server administrator.
SERVER_NAME	The canonical name of the current virtual host.
SERVER_ADDR	The IP address of the current virtual host.
SERVER_PORT	The port number from which the current request is being served.
SERVER_PROTOCOL	The version of the HTTP protocol being used to serve the request.
SERVER_SOFTWARE	This value can be configured using the ServerTokens configuration directive. At the most, it is the server software and version being used to serve the request, including any additional modules. At the least, it is simply the value Apache.

Continued

Table 5-1. *Continued*

Variable Name	Description
Date/Time Variables	
TIME_YEAR	The current year (e.g., 2006).
TIME_MON	The current month number, with January being 01, February being 02, and so on.
TIME_DAY	The current day of the month, with a leading zero.
TIME_HOUR	The current hour, in the range 00–23.
TIME_MIN	The current minute of the hour, in the range 00–59.
TIME_SEC	The current second component of the time, in the range 00–59.
TIME_WDAY	The day of the week, with 1 representing Monday.
TIME	The current date and time, in the format YYYYMMDDHHmmss.
Other Special Variables	
API_VERSION	The current version of the API, also referred to as the "mmn" number. This value is defined in include/ap_mmn.h and is primarily of interest to module developers.
THE_REQUEST	The full request sent by the browser to the server (e.g., GET /index.html HTTP/1.1).
REQUEST_URI	The resource requested in the HTTP request line. This is probably the variable you'll use most frequently. In the request example given for THE_REQUEST, the value of REQUEST_URI is /index.html.
REQUEST_FILENAME	The full path to the file being requested. Note that this is the same as the value of SCRIPT_FILENAME.
IS_SUBREQ	Contains the value true if the request being handled is a subrequest, and false otherwise.
HTTPS	Set to on if the request being handled is using SSL or TLS, and off otherwise.

Time-Based Redirection

For example, if you wished to serve different content to your visitors depending on the time of day, you may wish to do a conditional rewrite based on the time:

```
RewriteEngine on
RewriteCond    %{TIME_HOUR}%{TIME_MIN} >0700
RewriteCond    %{TIME_HOUR}%{TIME_MIN} <1900
RewriteRule    ^/page\.html$              page.day.html
RewriteRule    ^/page\.html$              page.night.html
```

This example demonstrates the use of more than one RewriteCond. Conditions chained together in this way are joined with an implicit AND—that is, both of the conditions must be satisfied in order for the RewriteRule to be run.

If both these conditions are satisfied, the rule is executed: page.html is rewritten to page.day.html.

The second RewriteRule is not affected by the conditions. Only the rule immediately following them is tied to them. In this case, the effect is that if the first rule is not executed, then the second one is. On the other hand, if the first rule is executed, then the second rule is run on the results of the first rule. That is to say, if page.html is rewritten to page.day.html, then the second rule will no longer match the request. The flowchart in Figure 5-1 may make this clearer.

It will be greatly instructive in your attempt to master mod_rewrite syntax if you will at this point pick several initial conditions (time is or is not in the given range, and the URL requested does or does not look like page.html) and then go through the flowchart. It is particularly important to remember that once you have rewritten the request from page.html to page.day.html, any future rewrite rules are performed on page.day.html and *not* on page.html.

One final note: The rules here are intended for use in either an .htaccess file or a <Directory> block. You can tell this is the case because of the lack of a leading slash on the rewrite pattern. In directory context (i.e., .htaccess files and <Directory> blocks), the file path is assumed and does not need to be specified.

The end result of this is that, between 0700 and 1900, requests for page.html get the document page.day.html, and those between 1900 and 0700 get page.night.html.

A similar technique may be used to serve different pages based on the browser type or based on the IP address of the visiting user.

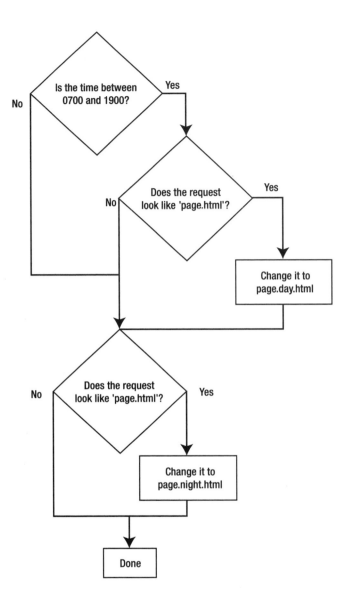

Figure 5-1. *Flow of a rewrite block*

RewriteCond Additional Variables

In addition to these mod_rewrite-specific variables, there are also three categories of additional variables that can be used in RewriteCond directives:

- Any environment variable can be used via the format %{ENV:variable-name}

- Any SSL environment variable can be used via the format %{SSL:variable-name}

- Any HTTP MIME request header can be used via the format %{HTTP:header-name}

Since all of the most useful of these variables are explicitly listed in Table 5-1, it is seldom necessary to use this extended variable format. However, it is occasionally useful. If, for example, you use SetEnvIf to define your own environment variables, it is handy to be able to use them in RewriteCond like regular environment variables. The following example is a variation on the ever-popular "don't steal my images" rules.

Image Theft

This example solves a common problem experienced by anyone with interesting or useful images on their website. Someone else, seeing those images, decides that they want to use them on their own website. So, they insert an image tag into their web page, pointing to the images on your web server.

This is problematic in two regards. The first is that the other person is violating your copyright by using your image on their website. The second is that they are using your bandwidth, rather than their own, to load content for their website. In any case, this is, in a sense, theft of your resources.

The goal, then, is to prevent anyone from loading your images, unless those images are embedded in a page on your own website. That is, you want the images to be forbidden unless the referer is something on your own website.

This problem can be solved using a rule set, as shown here:

```
SetEnvItNoCase Referer !\.rcbowen\.com not-linked-from-here-1
RewriteEngine On
RewriteCond %{ENV:not-linked-from-here} 1
RewriteRule \.(gif|jpg|png)$ /images/goaway.gif  [PT,NC]
```

In this rule set, the environment variable not-linked-from-here is set for any requests that do not contain rcbowen.com in the Referer variable. Later on, we check to see if that environment variable is set, and, if it is, we rewrite image requests to a "goaway" image. This has the effect of forbidding other sites from putting your images inline in their web pages.

A number of variations on this rule appear in Chapter 9.

RewriteCond Pattern

The second argument to RewriteCond—the pattern—is a PCRE, but there are a few other things you can put before this test pattern.

Comparison Tests

You may use comparison operators to test the value of the test string. In particular, you can use > (greater than), < (less than), or = (equal to) to compare the test string with some other value. You may ensure that a particular variable is undefined, or is set to an empty string, by checking that it is equal to "" (two quotation marks).

```
RewriteCond %{HTTP_HOST} = ""
```

Special Tests

The following special test flags may be applied to a test string:

- -d tests to see if the TestString exists as a file path and is a directory.

- -f tests to see if the TestString exists as a file path and is a file.

- -s tests to see if the TestString exists as a file path and has a size greater than zero.

- -l tests to see if the TestString exists as a file path and is a symbolic link.

- -F tests to see if the TestString is a valid file and is accessible through the existing access restriction and/or file permissions. This test does an HTTP subrequest, so it can be a big performance hit. Use it sparingly.

- -U tests to see if the TestString is a valid URL and is accessible through the existing access restrictions. This also does an HTTP subrequest and should be used sparingly.

Test Negation

Any of these tests can be negated (i.e., require that the condition fails to be met) by prefacing the pattern with an exclamation mark (!).

Examples

Now that you have more terms in your vocabulary, it's a good time to look at some examples of how you might use them.

The most useful example of these test flags involves using the -f and -d flags to determine whether or not a requested file exists. You might, for example, wish to rewrite all requests in a particular directory, but only if the requested file doesn't actually exist.

Consider, for example, the following scenario. You are migrating content from an old server to a new server. The old server is being retired. However, for some reason, you aren't able to move everything immediately, and so you have to migrate it gradually. Perhaps some of the content is being rewritten during the move to the new server.

So, in the meantime, you want to proxy all requests to the old server, if the file isn't found on the new server. This can be accomplished with some rewrite rules as follows:

```
RewriteEngine On

# Check to see if the file is there
RewriteCond %{RFQUEST_FILENAME} !-d
RewriteCond %{REQUEST_FILENAME} !-f
# If it's not, then proxy the request to the other server
RewriteRule (.*) http://oldserver.example.com$1 [P,L]
ProxyPassReverse / http://oldserver.example.com/
```

The RewriteCond lines check to see if the resource that was requested does in fact exist on the front-end server, either as a directory or as a file. If it doesn't, then the request is proxied through to the old server by the RewriteRule directive.

The ProxyPassReverse directive is there to ensure that any redirects issued by the back server appear to originate on the front server, so as not to confuse the browser.

It will likely be necessary to put in other RewriteCond directives to account for exceptions that must be made in the proxying, such as Alias and ScriptAlias directives, as well as any other handlers defined by Location directives.

RewriteCond Modifier Flags

Adding one or more flags can modify the way in which the matching is done. The available flags are as follows.

nocase

The nocase or NC flag specifies that the pattern in a RewriteCond is to be matched in a case-insensitive manner. Most environment variables and HTTP headers are case-insensitive, so there's way to tell ahead of time whether a particular value will be upper- or lowercase. It's safest to ask mod_rewrite to do case-insensitive matches if there's ever any chance that the case can be variable.

```
RewriteCond %{HTTP_REFERER} www.apache.org [NC]
```

This condition will return true if the referer contains www.apache.org, whether it is lowercase, uppercase, or mixed case.

ornext

The `ornext` or `OR` flag causes a chain of `RewriteCond` directives to be evaluated with a Boolean `OR`, rather than `AND`. That is, any of the conditions may be true, rather than requiring them all to be true, as is the default.

```
RewriteCond %{HTTP_REFERER} www.apache.org [NC,OR]
RewriteCond %{HTTP_REFERER} httpd.apache.org [NC]
RewriteRule …… (Rule will be evaluated if any of the above conditions is true)
```

Any number of conditions may be chained together in this manner. As you can see in this example, several flags may be combined for one rule.

Looping

One very common use for `RewriteCond` is to prevent looping. Looping occurs when the target of a `RewriteRule` matches the original pattern. When that happens, the rule can be executed again on the resulting URL, causing an infinite loop of rewrites. Using `RewriteCond` can break the loop before it has a chance to get started:

```
RewriteCond %{REQUEST_URI} !^/example\.html
RewriteRule ^/example /example.html [R]
```

This rule set causes any request starting with `example` to be redirected to `/example.html`. The resulting URL, however, starts with `example` and will therefore trigger the `RewriteRule` to be run again. The `RewriteCond` directive ensures that the rule will be skipped if the request is already for `example.html` and thus avoids this looping.

You'll know that you are in a looping situation when you get the error message "Redirection limit for this URL exceeded."

■**Note** By default, the redirection limit is set to 10, so that ten iterations through the loop will generate the "Redirection limit for this URL exceeded" error message. You can set this limit to something else by setting the `MaxRedirects` option to something else:

```
RewriteOptions MaxRedirects=20
```

Your browser may, in fact, enforce some other limit, too, which may not be related to the server-side limit in any way.

Always consider whether the target of your RewriteRule will cause the same rule to be executed again or some other rule to be triggered. Remember that rules operate on the result of prior rules, not on the value of the original request.

Summary

RewriteCond allows you to apply conditions to any RewriteRule. This allows you to be very granular in how RewriteRules are applied. A large number of options let you modify the behavior of the condition. It also allows you to prevent looping of a RewriteRule in the event that the target of the rule looks like the original pattern for the RewriteRule.

CHAPTER 6

■ ■ ■

The RewriteMap Directive

The RewriteMap directive lets you call on something external to help you do your rewriting. This can be a program, a database, or simply a file that lists the mappings. In this chapter, you'll learn how to use this directive, and you'll see a number of useful examples of the directive in action.

RewriteMap Syntax

The RewriteMap directive allows you to create a "function" that may be used later in RewriteCond and RewriteRule directives. The syntax of the function is as follows:

```
RewriteMap mapname maptype:maplocation
```

Once defined, this map may be used in any RewriteCond or RewriteRule directive:

```
RewriteRule (.*) ${mapname:$1| default}
```

The mapname is an arbitrary name that you make up. Think of it as a function name for the mapping that you're going to define. The maptype is, as you'll see in more detail shortly, one of several possible types, such as txt, rnd, dbm, int, or prg. The maplocation is where the particular mapping file or program is located or, in the case of int, what internal function is to be called.

A default value can be provided for the map, in the event that it doesn't return anything.

Map Types

The five types of maps that you can create with RewriteMap are shown in Table 6-1.

Table 6-1. *RewriteMap Map Types*

Map Type	Description
txt	A plain text file listing one-to-one mappings from keywords to values
rnd	A plain text file listing several alternatives for each keyword, from which a value will be randomly chosen
dbm	A DBM file containing one-to-one mappings in the format of the plain text file format
int	One of the available internal functions provided by mod_rewrite
prg	An external executable program that will be called by mod_rewrite and should return a mapping based on the data it receives via standard input (STDIN)

Each of these formats has its own little foibles, but the theory is the same: a call will be made to something external (with the exception if int, which is an internal function), giving it the argument pulled out of the RewriteRule. This mapping mechanism— whatever it is—will then return a response based on that argument, which will be used to construct the target of the rule.

txt Map Files

The simplest type of RewriteMap is a one-to-one mapping provided in a plain text file. That is, each line of the file contains two entries: the argument and the target to which that argument is to be mapped.

Such a map might be chosen in preference to having a large number of individual RewriteRules. While it offers no performance benefit over having a large number of RewriteRules, it is significantly easier to maintain, and so it can result in administration time savings. The map file itself, however, is plain text, and therefore unindexed, so it is not the fastest approach.

To create a text file RewriteMap, you should first create the map file itself. For the purpose of illustrating this technique, we'll construct a mythical URL redirection service. Specifically, we're going to have a site where requests for keywords are redirected to the appropriate portion of the Apache documentation. So, for example, a request for http://www.example.com/ apachedocs/allowoverride will be redirected to http://httpd.apache.org/docs/2.0/mod/ core.html#allowoverride. And any other Apache configuration directive will work the same way. Requesting http://www.example.com/apachedocs/*DIRECTIVE* will redirect to the official Apache documentation for that directive.

In order to do this, we create a text file containing a mapping from every Apache configuration directive to its place on the documentation site. Entries in this file will look like this:

```
allowoverride http://httpd.apache.org/docs/2.0/mod/core.html#allowoverride
authdbmuserfile ➡
http://httpd.apache.org/docs/2.0/mod/mod_auth_dbm.html#authdbmuserfile
bufferedlogs
http://httpd.apache.org/docs/2.0/mod/mod_log_config.html#bufferedlogs
```

and so on. The format is simple, with a keyword separated by a space from the value to which it will map.

We'll assume that this file is placed at /usr/local/apache/conf/documentation.map and use the following configuration directives to put this map in action:

```
RewriteEngine On
RewriteMap docmap txt:/usr/local/apache/conf/documentation.map
```

```
RewriteRule ^/apachedocs/(.*) \
    ${docmap:$1|http://httpd.apache.org/docs/2.0/mod/directives.html} [NE,R,L]
```

There's a lot going on here, so I'll go through it one line at a time.

In the first line of the example, the RewriteEngine gets turned on. This tells mod_rewrite that it is to honor upcoming rewrite statements. As you have probably already noticed by now, mod_rewrite ignores all rewrite statements in any scope where RewriteEngine is not turned On.

The next line defines the rewrite map. We've chosen the name docmap as the rule identifier, and in future RewriteRule statements, we need only refer to it by this name. It is a plain text mapping file, containing one-to-one definitions, as just shown. The full path to the rule file is supplied after the colon.

The RewriteRule looks for any requested URI starting with /apachedocs/ and intercepts the directive that it hopes to find in the URI following the /apachedocs/, putting it in $1.

Then comes the RewriteMap magic. Rather than supplying a replacement rule, we pass $1 to the rewrite map function defined by the RewriteMap rule.

```
${docmap:$1| http://httpd.apache.org/docs/2.0/mod/directives.html}
```

The second argument, after the pipe (|) character, is at least as important: it defines the default action if there is no result from the lookup in the docmap function. In our particular case, this means that if someone looks up a documentation keyword that doesn't actually exist, they will get sent instead to the list of valid directives, so that they can perhaps find whatever it was that they were looking for.

Finally, on the end of everything, we add a few flags to further clarify what is meant by the rule. The [NE] flag ensures that the # characters in the URLs are not escaped. Without the [NE], the # is converted to a %23, which in turn results in a 404 Not Found error once the request reaches the remote server.

The [R] flag indicates that the rewrite is a redirect. This is the default behavior when the target is a fully qualified URL (i.e., it includes http:// or https://), but it never hurts to be explicit, and it makes the rule easier to read when we are troubleshooting.

And the [L] tells the rewrite engine that we're all done, and it should go ahead and do the redirect now, rather than waiting to consult any further rules, if any.

If you are tempted to use the [NC] flag in this example, you'll be a little disappointed in the results. The lookup into the map file can't be case insensitive, unfortunately.

One final remark about this example is necessary, before we move on to discuss other map types. The rule itself is written to work in your main Apache configuration file (httpd.conf), and it will need to be changed to work in an .htaccess file. Specifically, if this rule is placed in an .htaccess file in the root document directory of your website, you will need to make the following changes:

- The RewriteMap directive must still go in your Apache configuration file. RewriteMap cannot go in .htaccess files.

- Make sure that the .htaccess file still contains the RewriteEngine On directive.

- The RewriteRule pattern needs to be ^(.*) instead of ^/(.*), because within the .htaccess file context, the leading slash has already been removed.

Randomized Rewrites

The next type of map, the rnd: map, allows for a result to be randomly selected from a list of several possible options. While there are a number of reasons for wanting to do this, we'll use the case of randomized rotation between several servers, for the purpose of load balancing.

In the example that follows, we'll be using this rewrite map file:

```
static mars|jupiter
dynamic venus|mercury|neptune|pluto
```

This file will be saved at the location /usr/local/apache/conf/servermap.rnd for the purpose of this example.

The idea here is that we have defined two groups of servers. One group, the "static" group, will be used to serve static files such as images. The other server will be used to serve the dynamically generated URLs. This allows us to have several low-end servers to serve the static files and then our high-powered servers to do the heavy lifting.

Our Apache configuration file uses the following configuration:

```
RewriteEngine On
RewriteMap servers rnd:/usr/local/apache/conf/servermap.rnd

RewriteRule ^/(.*\.(png|gif|jpg)) http://${servers:static}/$1 [NC,P,L]
RewriteRule ^/(.*) http://${servers:dynamic}/$1 [P,L]
```

The first two lines are the same as in the txt: example, except that the map type is now rnd: instead.

The next two lines rewrite all requests so that requests are proxied through to one of the two server pools. Requests ending in .png, .gif, or .jpg are forwarded via a proxy request to one of the static servers, which is randomly chosen from the list in the map file. All other requests are proxied to a server from the other pool.

Note that if there's content that you actually want to serve from the front-end server, you'll need to explicitly exclude that with RewriteCond rules placed before the RewriteRule line that would match it. For example, if you wanted the main site front page, index.html, served from the front-end machine, rather than having it proxied to the back-end servers, you would place this RewriteCond immediately before the second RewriteRule line:

```
RewriteCond %{Request_URI} !^/index.html
```

The effect of all of this is that the front-end server acts as a sort of load balancer—although the balancing is randomized—rather than doing any kind of real monitoring of the actual load on the back-end servers. You can think of it as a poor man's load balancer.

If one of the servers in the rotation is twice as powerful as the others, you may wish for it to get more of the requests than the other server. This can be accomplished by putting that server in the list more frequently:

```
dynamic venus|mercury|neptune|pluto|pluto
```

In the preceding entry from the servermap.rnd file, the server pluto appears twice, and thus will be statistically twice as likely to receive requests as the other servers.

Similarly, if one of the servers is down for maintenance and thus needs to be taken out of the rotation, you need only remove its name from the servermap.rnd file, and traffic will no longer be sent to it. This allows for servers to be added to and removed from the server pool in a completely transparent fashion.

The rnd: rewrite technique can also be used for other random things, such as displaying a random image in a web page. In your HTML, we can refer to a particular filename, such as, for example, random.gif:

```
<img src="/images/random.gif">
```

This would then trigger the following rewrite block:

```
RewriteMap randomimg rnd:/var/www/conf/image.map
```

```
RewriteEngine On
RewriteRule ^/images/random.gif  /var/www/images/${randomimg:random}.gif
```

The file `image.map` would contain a list of image names that could be substituted as the random image:

```
random monkey|pony|elephant|fish|puppy
```

Images can be added to or removed from this listing at will.

This technique has the added feature of concealing the actual name of the image file. If someone attempts to bookmark the image, or even if they right-click an image to save a local copy of it, they will not necessarily get the same image that they saw in the page.

This technique also allows proxy servers to cache the image, even though it is randomly served. The proxy server will not see the actual filename, but will only see `random.gif`, and will therefore cache the file with that URI. When using a more traditional random image mechanism, the proxy server would see each individual image filename instead and would cache each of those individually.

Hash-Type Maps

The previous two methods, particularly the first one, suffer from slowness. In the first example, we made a system where any Apache configuration directive would be rewritten to the documentation for that directive. This works well if your map file contains a few dozen directives. But if you try doing this with all of the configuration directives for all of the available Apache modules, as we did in the first example, you'll find that each page load takes an excessively long time to be rewritten.

This is because the rewrite file is plain text and unindexed. That means that every rewrite attempt requires mod_rewrite to read the file and walk through it one line at a time until it finds the line that matches. If that line happens to be the last one in the file, then mod_rewrite will have to read through the entire file, one line at a time, every time that URL is requested. As the file grows, so does the average time taken to do a rewrite.

The solution to this problem is to use an indexed file, such as a DBM file. This allows for much larger lists of rewrite mappings without any loss of performance. Using a `dbm:` map type allows you to do this.[1]

---

1. The `dbm:` map type, rather than the `txt:` map type, is what is being used to provide the documentation rewrite service described in the previous `txt:` section, at `http://fajita.drbacchus.com/`. So, if you point your browser to `http://fajita.drbacchus.com/allowoverride`, you will receive the Apache documentation for the `AllowOverride` configuration directive.

First, though, we need to generate that DBM file. We're going to create our map file in exactly the same way we did in the case of the txt: map files. That is, we'll have a list of keys and values, separated by one or more spaces. But once that map file is generated, we'll need to generate a DBM file from that map using the httxt2dbm utility:

```
httxt2dbm -i rewrite.map -o rewrite.dbm
```

Invoke httxt2dbm with no arguments to see more detailed instructions about how to use it:

```
httxt2dbm -- Program to Create DBM Files for use by RewriteMap
Usage: httxt2dbm [-v] [-f format] -i SOURCE_TXT -o OUTPUT_DBM

Options:
 -v    More verbose output

 -i    Source Text File. If '-', use stdin.

 -o    Output DBM.

 -f    DBM Format.  If not specified, will use the APR Default.
          GDBM for GDBM files (unavailable)
          SDBM for SDBM files (available)
          DB   for berkeley DB files (unavailable)
          NDBM for NDBM files (unavailable)
          default for the default DBM type
```

There are a number of different DBM formats, depending on the particular DBM library or libraries you happen to have installed. It is important that you use the same DBM library as was used to build Apache, so that the format is understandable to Apache.

If you are running a version of Apache that does not have the httxt2dbm utility available (any version before 2.0.56), there is a Perl program listing in the documentation that has a similar effect.

Once you've generated the DBM file, you can now point your RewriteMap directive at this newly created database with the following:

```
RewriteMap dbmrewritemap dbm:/path/to/rewrite.dbm
```

The dbmrewritemap rewrite "function" is now usable in RewriteRules:

```
RewriteRule /apachedocs/(.*) ${dbmrewritemap:$1} [R]
```

External Programs

Sometimes the rewrite that you want to do is sufficiently complicated that you just want to write a program to handle it for you. The prg: rewrite map type lets you do exactly that. The example given here will be in Perl, because Perl is exceptionally good at handling text string manipulation, but you can write a rewrite program in any language at all.

The syntax for using this map type is identical to the other map types. The file path points to the location of the script or program you wish to execute to perform the rewrite.

In the following example, we'll assume that someone copied a bunch of URLs incorrectly and replaced underscores with dashes in a brochure that talks about our website. In order to compensate for this typo, we'll need to make sure that the URLs in the brochure work, but also that the existing (correct) URLs all work, since existing links to our pages need to continue to work.

Doing this with just RewriteRules would be cumbersome. A URL might contain one dash or ten, and it's just easier to call on Perl to do this than try to monkey with [N] rules.

The script to do this translation in Perl is as follows:

```perl
#!/usr/bin/perl
$| = 1; # Turn off buffering
while (<STDIN>) {
    s/-/_/g; # Replace - with _ globally
    print $_;
}
```

Buffering is turned off so that the response is returned immediately. The program is started up when Apache starts up and is kept running for the lifetime of the Apache process. It is therefore important to keep our rewrite scripts as simple as possible. A rewrite program that hangs or crashes may cause the containing Apache process to wait indefinitely for a response and thus hang that particular child process.

To use this rewrite program, we'll use a configuration like the following. Assume that the program has been saved in a file called /usr/local/apache/conf/dash2score.pl.

```
RewriteEngine On
RewriteMap dash2score prg:/usr/local/apache/conf/dash2score.pl

RewriteRule (.*-.*) ${dash2score:$1} [PT]
```

The RewriteRule will get called for any URL containing a dash. It is possible that our publicist's typo is restricted to a smaller portion of the website, and we'll need to adjust the RewriteRule accordingly. The [PT] flag is used so that the resulting URL can be passed back to the URL mapping process, since we don't know what kind of URL we're dealing with.

The URI containing the dash is put into $1 and passed to the dash2score Perl script, which receives it on STDIN and rewrites it.

While this is an exceedingly simple example, external programs can do things arbitrarily complicated, such as looking up responses in a database or sending email when certain URL patterns are seen.

Internal Functions

In addition to writing your own rewrite maps, there are several internal functions that you can call in order to assist in your rewriting. These are available via the int: map type.

There are, at the time of this writing, four internal functions you can use in this way, as shown in Table 6-2.

Table 6-2. *Internal RewriteMap Function Names*

Function Name	Purpose
Toupper	Converts the argument to all uppercase characters
Tolower	Converts the argument to all lowercase characters
Escape	Converts any special characters in the argument to hex encoding
Unescape	Converts any hex-encoded characters back to the special characters they represent

Internal functions may be associated with a map name in the usual way, using the RewriteMap directive. While it is not required that you name the map the same as the function itself, that certainly makes things easier to remember:

```
RewriteMap tolower int:tolower
RewriteRule ^/articles/(.*)\.html /articles/${tolower:$1}.html [R]
```

This rule will rewrite requests for uppercase or mixed case filenames to the lowercase version of the same request.

Summary

The RewriteMap directive is greatly underused and is appropriate for many situations in which people have rule sets of dozens of RewriteRule directives. Maps may be one of five types—txt, rnd, dbm, prg, and int—and they may be used in any RewriteRule directive to assist in rewriting URLs.

CHAPTER 7

■ ■ ■

Basic Rewrites

Throughout the first several chapters of this book, you were exposed to numerous simple rewrite examples. Some of them were actually useful, while others existed purely to introduce concepts. This chapter takes a practical turn, in that the examples offered actually solve real-world problems. While not all of these will be directly applicable to you, working through the examples and their explanations will nonetheless provide you with a better understanding of what's involved in crafting rewrite solutions to problems that you experience on your own website.

Specifically, we'll discuss the following topics:

- *Adjusting URLs*: mod_rewrite gets used a lot to make ugly URLs less ugly, or perhaps easier to type, remember, and bookmark.

- *Renaming and reorganization*: When your website gets redesigned, mod_rewrite can help you make sure that all the existing bookmarks and links to your website keep working, while gradually moving people over to the new structure.

Adjusting URLs

The most common use of mod_rewrite appears to be adjusting URLs from one layout to another. This may be because the URLs on a site have been changed around for some reason, or perhaps it's because the site administrator believes that the URLs are too ugly and something else would be easier on the eyes.

We'll start with a simple example of this and then move on to some slightly more complex examples.

Problem: We Want to Rewrite Path Information to a Query String (Example 1)

We have a URL that looks like this: `http://example.com/vegetables.php?carrots`. We'd like it to look like this instead: `http://example.com/vegetables/carrots`.

Solution

```
RewriteEngine On
RewriteRule ^/vegetables/(.*) /vegetables.php?$1 [PT]
```

Discussion

The effect of this rule will be that anything appearing after /vegetables/ will be put into the query string. This is the simplest possible example of this class of rewrites, and it's almost always simpler than what you actually wanted to do. But it's a good starting place to see how you might approach something like this.

As always, if we are in fact using this in an .htaccess file, we need to remove the leading slash on the rule. It would therefore become

```
RewriteRule ^vegetables/(.*) vegetables.php?$1 [PT]
```

If you are trying to split off more arguments than just one, you will want to move on to the next example.

Problem: We Want to Rewrite Path Information to a Query String (Example 2)

We have a URL that looks like this: http://example.com/cgi-bin/book.cgi?author=➡ bowen&topic=modrewrite. We'd rather have it look like this: http://example.com/book/ bowen/modrewrite.

Solution

```
RewriteEngine On
RewriteRule ^/book/([^/]*)/([^/]*) \
/cgi-bin/book.cgi?author=$1&topic=$2 [PT]
```

Discussion

The solution here is an oversimplification on a couple of counts. In particular, it requires that the requested URL look exactly like the URL that is described in the pattern. That is, in this case, it must be /book/ followed by something, followed by slash, followed by something. If there are more (or fewer) "something"s, then the pattern won't match. The "something", in this case, is the pattern [^/]*, which means "some not-slash characters."[1]

---

1. Remember that in a character class, the ^ character means "not."

If you want a more flexible solution than this one, read on or consider using the RewriteMap directive discussed in Chapter 5.

Problem: We Want to Rewrite Path Information to a Query String (Example 3)

We have a URL that might have one, two, three, or four arguments, and we want to rewrite them to query string arguments. That is, we want URLs of the following form:

```
http://example.com/pets
http://example.com/pets/mammals
http://example.com/pets/mammals/dogs
http://example.com/pets/mammals/dogs/shorthaired
http://example.com/pets/mammals/docs/shorthaired/dachshunds
```

to be mapped internally to the following:

```
http://example.com/pets.php
http://example.com/pets.php?class=mammals
http://example.com/pets.php?class=mammals&family=dogs
http://example.com/pets.php?class=mammals&family=dogs&hair=shorthaired
http://example.com/pets.php?class=mammals&family=dogs&hair=shorthaired& ➥
species=dachshund
```

In each case, however, we want the URL displayed in the browser to appear as the original, not as the longer target URL.

Solution

We rewrite the URLs with the following rules, and then instruct the PHP file in question to ignore blank arguments:

```
RewriteEngine On
RewriteRule ^/pets/?([^/]*)/?([^/]*)/?([^/]*)/?([^/]*)/?  \
    /pets.php?class=$1&family=$2&hair=$3&species=$4 [PT]
```

Discussion

Although it would be possible, with a series of RewriteCond directives, to deal with each case individually, it's just not worth the effort. Most well-written code will deal gracefully with blank arguments, and it makes a lot more sense to do this processing in the PHP (or CGI, or whatever) than to try to do it in the RewriteRule, where it is far less efficient.

The rule that we're using here makes everything optional, starting with the first slash after pets, so any number of arguments will be sufficient. The question mark (?) character makes the slash itself optional, and the character class [^/] ("not slash") is optional by virtue of the *, which, as you recall, means "zero or more."

This is a good technique for handling a site that is hierarchical. As we proceed deeper into the URL structure of the website, each additional argument will be passed to the handling script.

Problem: We Have More Than Nine Arguments

Regular expressions (at least in the context of Apache mod_rewrite rules) limit us to $1 through $9. What if we have more than nine arguments?

Solution

Use RewriteMap with a prg: map type. Such a RewriteMap program would need to loop over the entire contents of the string and process it sequentially. A simple example of such a RewriteMap follows.

In the configuration file, we might have the following:

```
RewriteMap manyargs prg:/bin/splitargs
RewriteEngine On
RewriteRule ^/pets/(.*)$ /pets.php?${manyargs:$1} [PT]
```

while /bin/splitargs itself would be something like this:

```
#!/usr/bin/perl
$|=1;
my $i=0;
my @args = split !/!, $_;
foreach my $arg (@args) {
    $i++;
    $return .= "&arg$i=$arg";
}
$return =~ s/^&//;
print $return;
```

This rule set will allow for an arbitrary number of arguments to appear on the URL line and will generate a query string with those arguments named sequentially.

Discussion

There's no way to have a $10, for the simple reason that $10 is indistinguishable from $1 followed by a 0. Thus, it would be unclear whether we are attempting to use the variable $1 or the variable $10 in the context of a rewrite expression. So, if we want more than nine backreferences in our `RewriteRule`, we're going to have to bring out the big guns and use a `RewriteMap` program. Within a `RewriteMap`, we can do whatever transforms we like without regard to a limited number of arguments.

Note See Chapter 6 for in-depth coverage of `RewriteMap`.

Renaming and Reorganization

Another common use for mod_rewrite is to change the name of pages, or portions of a website, without having existing links to the site suddenly become invalid.

Usually, this can be done with the `Redirect` directive, but in the case of a sitewide change, `Redirect` can become cumbersome. Also, there is often a requirement (or at least a desire) that the end user not be made aware of the change, by virtue of seeing the URL change in their browser address bar, and so mod_rewrite must be called on to make the redirection invisible.

The next few recipes show a few variations on this theme, and then we'll move on to look at rules that deal with having the "right" server name, for some definition of "right." There are a variety of reasons for requiring a particular server name, ranging from cookies to SSL to vanity, and the rules presented here enforce that choice.

Problem: We've Switched from ColdFusion to PHP, but We Want All Old URLs to Continue Working

We've done a page-for-page migration of our website from CFM files to PHP files. The old URLs should continue to work because people have bookmarked them.

Solution

```
RewriteEngine On
RewriteRule (.*)\.cfm $1.php [PT,L]
```

Discussion

If we actually want to have the URL change in the browser to the new nomenclature, then we should replace the PT with an R. This will result in a round-trip back to the browser, and the user will see in their address bar (if they notice) the new URL and have an opportunity to bookmark the new address in preference to the old one.

$1 will contain the entire URI, including any directory path information. Only the final file extension will be changed. Any query string information that had been passed to the original URL will also be retained, which is behavior that we would not get if we had used a simple Redirect or RedirectMatch directive.

Problem: We're Looking in More Than One Place for a File

In the course of rearranging our website, we split our image files between two directories. It seemed like a good idea at the time, but there are two different places that files could have ended up. We want to look in both places when a file is requested.

Solution

```
<Directory /usr/local/apache/htdocs/images>
RewriteEngineOn
RewriteCond %{REQUEST_FILE} !-f
RewriteRule (.*)  /pictures/$1 [R,L]
</Directory>
```

Discussion

Frequently, when people ask questions of this nature in various support forums, such as mailing lists, IRC, or newsgroups, the answer that they receive is "You really should fix your directory structure instead." That is, of course, a good answer. However, as we all know, there are situations where it's not quite that easy.

The -f test checks to see if the file is in the requested location. If it's not, then we move on to the RewriteRule, and the image is requested from the other location instead. This process could be continued with another rewrite rule set in that other directory, too, if the problem was bigger than just two alternate locations.

The long-term solution is to figure out which image references are pointing the wrong place and fix them.

Problem: Some of Our Content Is on Another Server

In a slightly more involved version of the previous example, we've split our content between two web servers. For example, perhaps we've put images on one server and the rest of our content on another, in an effort to balance the load between two servers. This, too, seemed like a good idea, but some people have bookmarks and aren't ending up on the right server.

Solution

Rewrite failing requests to the other server:

```
RewriteEngine On
RewriteCond %{REQUEST_URI} !-U
RewriteRule (.*) http://other.example.com$1 [R]
```

Discussion

The -U test is rather time-consuming. It checks ahead of time whether the requested URI will result in a Not Found request. This includes traversing Aliases, UserDirs, and other URL mapping functions. While this takes longer than simply doing a -f check, it is also far more robust, as a -f check will only look for files within the document directory.

Problem: We Require a Canonical Hostname

Although there are several possible hostnames that can be used to reach our website, we want to require that everyone use one in particular.

Solution

```
RewriteEngine On
RewriteCond %{HTTP_HOST} !^www\.example\.com$ [NC]
RewriteRule (.*) http://www.example.com$1 [R,L]
```

Discussion

It is extremely common for people to copy this recipe incorrectly and end up with exactly the opposite of what they want. It is therefore very important to understand what this recipe is actually saying.

The RewriteCond says, "If the requested host is *NOT* www.example.com..." The RewriteRule then says, "...then redirect the request to www.example.com."

So, if we are modifying this for use on our server, we'll replace www.example.com in both the RewriteCond and the RewriteRule with the hostname that we want to force everyone to use. In the RewriteCond, the dots are escaped because it is a regular expression. In the RewriteRule, they are not, because it is a literal target string.

The [NC] on the RewriteCond allows people to use an uppercase (or mixed-case) version of the hostname. If you wish to be even more restrictive than that, you can remove the [NC] and be just as controlling as you want.

Problem: We're Viewing the Wrong SSL Host

As you may be aware, you're able to have only one SSL host per IP address. This causes a problem if you have multiple name-based hosts on that same IP address. Someone going to https://other.example.com/ may end up getting the content from https://www.example.com/ and be rather confused.

We want to make sure that if someone asks for an HTTPS connection to the wrong hostname, they get sent back to the HTTP version of that hostname.

Solution

```
<VirtualHost  10.7.14.9:443>
...
RewriteEngine On
RewriteCond %{HTTP_HOST} !^www\.example\.com$
RewriteRule (.*) http://%{HTTP_HOST}$1 [R,L]
...
</VirtualHost>
```

Discussion

Because the rewrite happens after the SSL connection has already been negotiated, the user will probably still receive the browser warning about getting the wrong SSL certificate. This will likely be a little confusing. However, we won't end up with them at the wrong SSL host, as they'll get redirected as soon as the SSL handshake is done.

Note that this rule set goes inside the SSL virtual host. Putting it elsewhere will likely cause it to be ignored.

Problem: We Need to Force SSL

We want to ensure that access to a certain site, or to a particular part of a certain site, is always via SSL.

Solution

```
RewriteEngine On
RewriteCond %{HTTPS} !=on
RewriteRule ^(.*) https://%{SERVER_NAME}$1 [R,L]
```

Or, use the following for just a particular directory:

```
RewriteEngine On
RewriteCond %{HTTPS} !=on
RewriteRule ^secure(.*) https://%{SERVER_NAME}secure$1 [R,L]
```

Discussion

This rule set is intended to be placed in an .htaccess file, in order to redirect requests to the HTTPS version of the same site. In the event that we have access to the main server configuration file, such a rewrite would be unnecessary, since we could simply put a Redirect directive in the non-SSL virtual host.

However, when we are restricted to using .htaccess files for configuration, we often need to jump through a few hoops to do simple things. If HTTP and HTTPS are being served out of the same directory, then a simple Redirect directive will wind up causing a redirect loop. However, with this rewrite rule set, we first check to see if we're already in SSL mode, and we perform the redirect only if we're not.

Finally, note that the SSLRequireSSL directive, which is available in mod_ssl, denies non-SSL access to a particular scope, but it does not cause a redirect to an SSL-enabled access if a non-SSL access is attempted.

Summary

Although your particular rewrite needs are likely to be different from the ones shown in this chapter, the techniques listed here should be helpful in teaching you to craft your own rewrite expressions. And, of course, there's also a pretty good chance that at least one of the recipes presented in this chapter is something that you will encounter at some point.

CHAPTER 8

■ ■ ■

Conditional Rewrites

In Chapter 5, we talked about the RewriteCond directive and how you might use it to make rewrites conditional. In this chapter, you'll see a variety of examples that use this functionality to accomplish a number of common tasks and a few not-so-common tasks.

One example was given in Chapter 5, and I'll elaborate on that. Other examples were hinted at, and I'll cover those in detail here.

Looping

Although looping was discussed in Chapter 5, it is worth mentioning again here, as it is perhaps the most common example of the use of conditional rewrites.

Many uses of mod_rewrite create conditions where the rewrite will loop. That is, the rewrite will occur repeatedly until either the browser or the server decides that something has gone awry and returns a "redirection limit exceeded" error message.

As one simple example of this, consider the situation where we have a website that is temporarily down for maintenance, and the administrator thinks it would be a good idea to redirect everything to a page explaining that the site is temporarily down:

```
RewriteEngine On
RewriteRule (.*) /maintenance.html [R]
```

This seems simple enough, except for one small problem. When a browser requests any URI on the server—for example, /index.html—this RewriteRule sends a redirect back to the browser, which then requests the URI /maintenance.html. This request triggers the RewriteRule, which matches, and redirects the browser to /maintenance.html. That request, in turn, gets redirected to /maintenance.html, and so on, forever—or at least until the "redirection limit exceeded" condition is reached. This is referred to as a *looping rewrite rule*, because the rewrite target matches the rewrite pattern.

There are a few different ways to address this problem. The simplest of these is to impose a rewrite condition on the rewrite rule. Expressed in English, this would be "Redirect to /maintenance.html unless you're already there."

```
RewriteEngine On
RewriteCond %{REQUEST_URI} !^/maintenance.html
RewriteRule (.*) /maintenance.html [R]
```

The RewriteCond compares the variable %{REQUEST_URI}—that is, the URI requested by the browser—to the negated pattern ^/maintenance.html. Thus, the rule will be applied only if the request does not start with /maintenance.html.

Since it's been a few chapters since this was mentioned, it is worth repeating here that things are slightly different if you're putting these rules in an .htaccess file. In particular, the directory prefix is removed from the %{REQUEST_URI} variable, as all requests are automatically assumed to be relative to the current directory. So, if you were to have this same rewrite block in an .htaccess file in your document root directory, it would appear instead as follows:

```
RewriteEngine On
RewriteCond %{REQUEST_URI} !^maintenance.html
RewriteRule (.*) /maintenance.html [R]
```

In case you can't immediately see what the difference is, it's the missing / on the front of the RewriteCond pattern.

Again, there are a few different ways to address the problem. Another method involves expressing the rule set as a file path. As you can see from the preceding example, the rule set presented uses a [R] flag, indicating that the target is a URI to which we want to redirect. The default behavior of RewriteRule is to treat the target as a file path. Thus, if we don't want to generate a redirect, we can express the rule set as follows:

```
RewriteEngine On
RewriteRule (.*) /var/www/html/maintenance.html [L]
```

Since this is a file path rewrite, the target URI does not get sent back to the URL mapping phase, and so the rewrite rule doesn't have a chance to loop. The [L] flag (Last) ensures that the rule is run immediately, rather than having a chance to consider other rewrite rules that may be in effect in the same scope.

And as before, things are slightly different when the rule appears in an .htaccess file, because everything is assumed to be relative to the current directory:

```
RewriteEngine On
RewriteRule (.*) maintenance.html [L]
```

I'll make one final remark about this rule before moving on. The purists among you[1] have likely been grumbling throughout this example about the (.*) pattern in this

---

1. And probably my tech editor, too!

`RewriteRule`. It's not necessary, and it's inefficient. Rest assured that I included it here so that I could make this remark.

It would have been far more efficient, on two counts, to simply write the rule as follows:

```
RewriteRule . maintenance.html [L]
```

This will cause a redirect if the pattern . matches the requested URI. That is, it will match on the first character of the request and stop there.

The .* pattern, on the other hand, will run to the end of the string, matching every character. Thus, it will take considerably longer to run. Additionally, since we have enclosed .* in parentheses, it will also capture the result in the variable $1, which we don't use, and so it is consuming additional time and memory for no particular purpose.

The moral of this story is that whenever you either use a repetition character or capture a result in parentheses for use as a backreference, you should consider whether this is really necessary or unneeded overhead.

As a further example of this kind of waste, you will frequently see .*$ mistakenly applied to the end of a regular expression, for example:

```
RewriteRule ^/images.*$ - [F]
```

This example causes a Forbidden message to be returned for any request for a URI starting with /images. However, the rest of the regular expression (the .*$ on the end) is nothing more than wasted time. The regular expression engine will run out to the very end of the string matching additional characters, which it is then going to ignore. A pattern match of ^/images is completely sufficient for the task at hand.

Date- and Time-Based Rewrites

It's ideal to demonstrate date and time conditional rewrites using a problem-solution format, since they're fairly simple. We'll next expand on the example given in Chapter 5.

Problem: We Want to Show a Competition Website Only During a Competition

In Chapter 5, the example given was a time-based rewrite, where one page was provided during the day and a different one during the night. In this section, we'll consider the example where we wish to show a particular page on our website during a particular date range—for example, for a competition or a special promotion that we are offering on the site—and then have it go away when the competition is over.

Let's make this just a little more complicated. Suppose we want people coming to our website to see the competition page, but, after they've seen it, we don't really want to bother them with it again. This will require two conditionals: the date-based one and the test to see if the users have been here before.

Solution

```
RewriteEngine On
RewriteCond %{TIME} > 20050701080000
RewriteCond %{TIME} < 20050705170000
RewriteCond %{HTTP_COOKIE} !frontdoor=yes
RewriteRule /index.html  /contest.html \
    [R,CO=frontdoor:yes:.apacheadmin.com:1440,L]
```

Discussion

Like the example in Chapter 5, we start by checking the current date and seeing if it falls in a particular range. In this case, by using the %{TIME} variable, we can get down-to-the-second accuracy and check for a particular date and time.

Next, we check to see if the user has already come in through the front door. We do this by checking for the presence of a cookie called frontdoor with a value of yes.

Finally, if all of these conditions pass, we move on to the RewriteRule, in which we redirect requests for /index.html to /contest.html instead. The RewriteRule also sets a cookie, which will cause the third RewriteCond to fail the next time this user comes to the site. In this case, we're setting the cookie for 1,440 minutes, which is 24 hours. This will cause the user to see the contest page again tomorrow when they come back to the site, but it won't make them see it more than once a day.

RewriteCond conditions are additive by default. That is to say, they are implicitly AND conditions, and all three conditions must be satisfied for the following RewriteRule to be applied. Note that it would still be possible to get to the /contest.html page outside of the contest dates range, and you may wish to explicitly protect against this.

```
RewriteEngine On
RewriteCond %{TIME} < 20050701080000
RewriteCond %{TIME} > 20050705170000
RewriteRule /contest.html - [F]
```

This will return a 403 Forbidden response before and after the contest, so that you don't have to get up in the middle of the night to modify the site content. It might be more useful, and less jarring to users, to rewrite that request to an informative page telling them that the contest is over and that they should try again next year.

```
RewriteEngine On
RewriteCond %{TIME} < 20050701080000
RewriteCond %{TIME} > 20050705170000
RewriteRule /contest.html /contest-over.html [R]
```

Redirecting Based on Client Conditions

There are a wide variety of variables passed to you by the browser, and any of them can be used in rewrite rules and conditions.

Problem: We Want to Redirect Users Based on Their Browser Type

In this example, we'll send people to different pages based on the browser that they are using. There are a variety of reasons for wanting to do this. Certain techniques work in one browser and not in another, and so you may wish to deliver different content based on which browser is being used. Or perhaps you have an ideological reason for wishing to forbid entrance to people using a particular browser. In either case, the technique is the same.

Solution

```
RewriteCond %{HTTP_USER_AGENT} MSIE [NC]
RewriteRule /index.html /msie_index.html [L,R]
RewriteCond %{HTTP_USER_AGENT} Safari [NC]
RewriteRule /index.html /safari_index.html [L,R]
# Everybody else seems to call themselves Mozilla
RewriteRule /index.html /moz_index.html [L,R]
```

Discussion

What you're actually trying to do with this rule set will, of course, affect exactly what you do with the rules. In this case, there are three versions of the page. There's one for Microsoft Internet Explorer, one for Apple Safari, and one for everybody else.

Problem: We Want to Send External Users Elsewhere

In this scenario, we'd like to block access to parts of our site from outside visitors, but send them somewhere else, rather than simply giving them a Forbidden page.

Solution

```
RewriteEngine On
RewriteCond %{REMOTE_ADDR} !^192.168
RewriteRule ^/internal http://www.example.com/ [R,L]
```

Discussion

This is another case when using mod_rewrite is probably overkill, and a simpler and more efficient solution is available.

```
Order deny,allow
Deny from all
Allow from 192.168
ErrorDocument 403 http://www.example.com/
```

In either case, the user gets redirected to the front page of the site (or to some other site, perhaps). We can, however, use the mod_rewrite solution in conjunction with other rewrites, or perhaps to set various environment variables or cookies.

What is perhaps more interesting is to give different content entirely to internal and external viewers, for example:

```
RewriteEngine On
RewriteCond %{REMOTE_ADDR} ^192\.168
RewriteRule (.*) /var/www/internal$1 [L]
RewriteRule (.*) /var/www/external$1 [L]
```

This effectively defines two virtual hosts, one of which is seen by the internal viewers and the other of which is seen by the external viewers.

Problem: We Want to Serve Different Content Based on the User's Username

This problem turns out to be rather harder than it seems at first. We want to have users log in, and then we want to serve different content based on the username that the user supplied.

Solution

```
RewriteEngine On
RewriteCond %{LA-U:remote_user} !^$
RewriteRule ^/private(.*)  /home/%{LA-U:remote_user}/public_html$1

<Location /private>
    AuthType Basic
    AuthName "Personal content"
    AuthUserFile /www/conf/passwd
    Require valid-user
</Location>
```

Discussion

Although this initially seems very easy, searching online for this kind of solution will reveal many people who gave it up as impossible. The source of the problem is that rewrite rules are run before the authentication phase, so we can't know what the username is until it's too late. The %{LA-U:variable} syntax gives us a way around this stalemate, by doing a look-ahead for what the value of that variable will be once we get there. This is, of course, rather slow, but since there's no other way to get what we want, we have to put up with that.

The advantage of this approach is that we can give out one URL to all of our users, and it will magically give them the right content based on their login information.

The RewriteCond there, while it may initially appear to be unnecessary, forces the initial authentication. Without this, the rewrite happens with a null username, and we end up being sent to /home//public_html/ and getting a Forbidden message. The RewriteCond causes the rule to be skipped, and the authentication is performed. Once that happens, the rule gets run the second time through, and everything works smoothly.

Problem: We Want to Force Users to Come Through the Front Door

We want to ensure that all accesses to our website first visit the front page of the site.

Solution

```
RewriteEngine On
RewriteCond %{HTTP_COOKIE} !frontpage=yes
RewriteRule .* /index.html  [R,L]
RewriteRule /index.html - [CO=frontdoor:yes:.apacheadmin.com]
```

Discussion

This is, of course, just a variation on one of the earlier recipes in this chapter. Many websites, for whatever reason, force all of their users to enter through the front page. Personally, I think that this is annoying, and that deep linking is a tribute to the usefulness of your website. Forcing people through the front page merely makes it harder for users to get the information that they came for. But this recipe provides the means, without endorsing the desire itself.

On every request, the RewriteCond checks for the presence of a cookie indicating that the user has been through the front page. In the event that the cookie has not been set, the request is redirected to the front page of the site. Once the user has been to the front page of the site, any other requests will not generate the redirect, since the cookie is already set.

This will, of course, break any bookmarks or direct links for anyone who has not first visited the front page.

Problem: We Want to Prevent Users from Uploading PHP Files to an Unload Area and Then Executing Them

Any time you permit the uploading of files to any portion of your website, someone will attempt to take advantage of this to exploit your server. It's inevitable, and you need to take proactive steps to prevent this from causing damage to your server.

The technique supplied here will work for a variety of different file types once you understand why it works. In particular, you want to prevent PHP files from being uploaded, because these files might contain malicious code.

Solution

```
RewiteEngine On
RewriteCond %{REQUEST_METHOD} ^PUT$ [OR]
RewriteCond %{REQUEST_METHOD} ^MOVE$
RewriteRule ^/dav/(.*)\.php /dav/$1.nophp
```

Discussion

Files that are uploaded to the /dav section of our website (you'll need to modify this to point to whatever portion of your site where you're permitting upload) with a .php file extension are created instead with a .nophp file extension, rendering them inoperable. Likewise, if someone attempts to rename an existing file to have a .php extension, this rename operation will result in the file being renamed to have a .nophp extension instead.

Many well-known exploits involve this type of two-step attack, where a file is first uploaded and then executed. Preventing the initial upload goes a long way toward completely blocking these types of attacks.

Problem: The Client Certificate Validation Error Message Is Indecipherable

To ordinary people, when they receive an error message telling them that their SSL client certificate failed validation, the message is cryptic and not very helpful. We'd like to provide a more detailed and understandable error message when this happens.

Solution

```
SSLVerifyClient Optional
RewriteEngine On
RewriteCond %{SSL_CLIENT_VERIFY} !="SUCCESS"
RewriteRule .* /path/client-cert-error.html [L]
```

Discussion

Because RewriteCond can inspect any server or environmental variable, we can check to see if the client verification passed or failed by looking at the SSL_CLIENT_VERIFY variable. If it is not set to SUCCESS, we know it failed, and we redirect requests to a detailed page telling the end user what happened and what they can do to fix it or who to contact for further details.

Ordinarily, we would handle the custom error message causing the ErrorDocument directive, but in this case, there is not a distinct error message associated with this error condition, so we have to look for some other indicator of the error.

Summary

Any environmental conditions can be used to decide whether or not to run a RewriteRule. This allows you to be very creative in your rewriting and to make URLs magically do the right thing under different conditions.

CHAPTER 9

■ ■ ■

Access Control

In this chapter, we consider the issue of using mod_rewrite to solve access control problems.

Access control is the term given to any technique used to determine who is allowed into your website and who is kept out. This can be based on any criteria, from the IP address of the browser, to the time of the day, or any other criteria that occurs to you.

Before we jump into doing access control with mod_rewrite, we'll look at some alternate ways to accomplish the same things, and discuss the advantages and disadvantages of each. As I've pointed out a number of times in other chapters, people do have the tendency to use mod_rewrite when a more efficient—and often easier—solution may be implemented using other modules.

There are, of course, times when mod_rewrite is the right answer, but you generally want to consider it a last resort, rather than the first tool you reach for.

When Not to Use mod_rewrite

Apache provides a variety of tools for access control based on client IP address or any other available environment variable. Because using mod_rewrite will cause performance degradation, you should consider using these other tools before you look to mod_rewrite.

Address-Based Access Control

If you are performing simple address-based access control, doing so using the allow and deny directives is the easiest and most efficient approach:

```
<Directory /www/protected>
    Order allow,deny
    Allow from all
    Deny from 172.20.
</Directory>
```

This will deny access to the /www/protected directory to anyone from the 172.20 network, but allow access to anyone outside of it.

If you are using an .htaccess file, this exact effect would be reproduced by placing the .htaccess file in the directory /www/protected and putting this same block in there, without the <Directory> and </Directory> lines. That is, the file would contain only these lines:

```
Order allow,deny
Allow from all
Deny from 172.20.
```

This approach can be made more flexible, but still more efficient than using mod_rewrite, by using the <LocationMatch> or <DirectoryMatch> directives to apply the rule set to a wider range of URIs or directories.

For example, if you wished to deny access to URIs starting with a or b, you could accomplish this with the following configuration:

```
<LocationMatch ^/[aAbB]>
      order allow,deny
      Allow from all
      Deny from 172.20.
</LocationMatch>
```

A mod_rewrite-based approach will be demonstrated later, and you are encouraged to implement both and perform benchmarks of each approach.

Environment Variable–Based Access Control

In addition to the IP address, other environment variables are available to the access control mechanism, either directly via the deny from env= or allow from env= syntax or indirectly using SetEnvIf. If, for example, you wanted to deny access to users who are not using Firefox, you could use the following:

```
SetEnvIfNoCase User-Agent !firefox otherbrowser
Order allow,deny
Allow from all
Deny from env=otherbrowser
```

The advantages of this approach over using mod_rewrite to accomplish the same task are a reduction in complexity and an improvement in performance.

<Directory> BLOCKS AND .htaccess FILES

The general rule for .htaccess files and <Directory> blocks is that anything that can be put in a <Directory> block can be replaced by those same configuration lines placed in an .htaccess file in that directory. That is, any time you have the following:

```
<Directory /something>
   ConfigurationLinesHere
</Directory>
```

that functionality will be duplicated by placing an .htaccess file in the directory /something containing only this line:

```
ConfigurationLinesHere
```

Bear in mind that some directives are not permitted at all in .htaccess files, and the AllowOverride configuration directive must be set appropriately in order to permit certain things in .htaccess files. And, in particular in the case of mod_rewrite, there are subtle syntax changes when rules are put in .htaccess files.

The reverse is also true: anything you can put in an .htaccess file can be put instead into a <Directory> block in the main configuration file.

Access Control with mod_rewrite

Having shown some ways to accomplish tasks without mod_rewrite and telling you these ways are faster, it's only fair that I also show you how to do the same things with mod_rewrite. At the very least, this gives you a way to compare and see if my claims are accurate.

Earlier, you saw the non-mod_rewrite way to do address-based access control. In this section, I'll show both examples again, but done with mod_rewrite. First, we'll look at the more common task of denying access to a particular directory to clients from a particular network. Then, we'll deny access to several directories at once.

Problem: We Want to Deny Access to a Particular Directory

Here, we'd like to deny access to a directory to clients from the 172.20 network, using mod_rewrite. We'll do this several different ways, so that you can see some of the alternative approaches available. Please keep in mind that we've already established that it's probably best, in most cases, to do this without the assistance of mod_rewrite at all.

However, there may be cases where you want to combine these techniques with a larger rule set to accomplish something more complex.

Solution

```
<Directory /www/restricted>
    RewriteEngine On
    RewriteCond %{REMOTE_ADDR} ^172\.20\.
    RewriteRule .*? - [F]
</Directory>
```

Discussion

Functionally, this is no different from the deny from 172.20 directive we used in the non-mod_rewrite implementation. Clients whose address starts with 172.20 will receive a Forbidden message when they attempt to access content in this directory, as desired. This implementation takes a lot longer, though, since a regular expression has to be applied to the remote client's address as well as to the requested URI itself.

While I'm against this particular approach, it's worth using this example to demonstrate a few important concepts that have been alluded to already. First, it's important to note that the regular expression for the remote address is ^172\.20\. and not merely 172.20. Using a regular expression of just 172.20 would also match the address 208.172.204.9 because it contains 172.20 as a substring. And ^172\.20 would also match 172.20.209.44, for example.

Second, and most important, I want to draw your attention to the RewriteRule. The regular expression to which we are comparing the request is .*?, which will match as little as possible. As mentioned in Chapter 2, regular expressions are "greedy" by default and will try to match as much as possible. By using the ? syntax, we match as little as possible, in order to save time and effort. The less we have to match, the more efficient the expression will be.

As you experiment with regular expressions, and encounter regular expressions that other people have written, you will frequently encounter rewrite rules that use .* or even (.*) or ^.*$ when they really only need to use . instead. While this seems like a rather small matter, as your understanding of regular expressions grows, you'll realize that it's not a small matter at all.

The regular expression .* forces the regex engine to look at the entire string, all the way to the last character, comparing each character to the wildcard character . to see if it matches. Of course, it will match. This means that for a string of n characters, n comparisons must be made.

If you use the pattern .*? rather than the pattern .* to mean "any string," you will have to make only a single comparison, or perhaps no comparison at all, since an empty string matches this pattern as well. This causes a significant performance improvement. Since only a single comparison is made, you will have the same execution time regardless of the length of the requested URI, whereas a comparison string of .* will take progressively longer the longer the requested URI is.

The general rule to remember is that you want to find the simplest possible regular expression that will match the desired string, not the most complete one. Never use .* when . will suffice, and never gratuitously tack .*$ onto the end of a regular expression.

Problem: We Want to Deny Access to Several Directories at Once

Restricting access to a large number of directories can be tedious if you have to manually restrict each one. However, there's an effective way to restrict several with just a few directives, as demonstrated here.

Solution

```
RewriteEngineOn
RewriteCond %{REMOTE_ADDR} ^172\.20\.
RewriteRule ^/[abAB] - [F]
```

Discussion

Hopefully I've already made clear that the preceding code isn't the right way to do this. You should use <LocationMatch> or a <DirectoryMatch> and a Deny directive, as discussed earlier. However, this rule set does illustrate how to do access control based on an arbitrary URL pattern.

You can, of course, combine the two methods, if desired:

```
<LocationMatch ^/[abAB]>
    RewriteCond %{REMOTE_ADDR} ^172\.20\.
    RewriteRule .*? - [F]
</LocationMatch>
```

This has the same effect, but it's harder to read.

Since <Directory>, <DirectoryMatch>, <Location>, and <LocationMatch> cannot be used in .htaccess files, some creative combination of these methods may be required to get this working in an .htaccess file.

A further subtle difference between the RewriteCond approach and the <DirectoryMatch> approach is that the RewriteCond will match any URI starting with as or bs, whereas the <DirectoryMatch> will only match a directory. If it's particularly important to you that the target is a directory, you could force this:

```
RewriteCond %{REQUEST_FILENAME} ^/[abAB][^/]*/
```

This approach requires that the requested URI map to a directory path starting with a, b, A, or B, followed by zero or more nonslash characters, followed by a slash. This guarantees that it is a directory name, rather than a file, that happens to start with one of those letters.

And, finally, I have one more remark about possible alternate approaches. Rather than using the [abAB] character class, you could instead use [ab] and then append a [NC] flag on the end of the RewriteCond to make the condition case insensitive.

Simple Client-Based Access Control

Sometimes you'll want to control access based on user behavior. This section demonstrates how mod_rewrite can play an important role in preventing abuse of your website.

Problem: We Want to Block a Spider from Hammering Our Website

More specifically, we want to block a client from our website if they're connecting using a particular user agent. While this might be used to block users who have a particular browser, as suggested in the last chapter, we're going to use it for a more common problem. We have a particular robot (or *bot*, or *spider*) that is hammering our website, and we want to block its access to our site.

There are a number of ways to approach this. We'll start with a simple rewrite-based solution.

Solution

```
RewriteEngine On
RewriteCond %{USER_AGENT} evilbot [NC]
RewriteRule . - [F]
```

Discussion

This is the simplest possible approach. If the user agent looks like "evilbot," then we're going to forbid their access to any URL. The regular expression . matches any nonempty request, and the [F] flag returns a 403 Forbidden status response. What could be easier?

However, there may be a better way to approach this. Just because you can do something with mod_rewrite doesn't mean you should. So let's take a look at an alternate approach.

```
SetEnvIf  User-Agent evilbot go-away
<Directory /var/www/>
    Order allow,deny
    Allow from all
    Deny from env=go-away
</Directory>
```

This block of configuration accomplishes exactly the same thing, but without invoking mod_rewrite. The obvious question is whether it's actually a "better" way to do it, for some definition of "better." While the common wisdom is that avoiding mod_rewrite will necessarily lead to better performance, this turns out not always to be the case, and so you may wish to do some benchmarks comparing the two approaches.

In this particular case, the RewriteRule approach turned out to be slightly slower, in my tests. The benchmarks that I did had the RewriteRule trailing by 10 percent.

The advantage of the RewriteRule, in this case, might be a greater flexibility or the ability to combine these criteria with other rules also being run. However, if the only consideration is the User-Agent type, then it is more efficient to use the SetEnvIf approach.

As always, when doing any kind of access control based on user agent strings, it's important to remember that it is very easy to change the reported user agent string and get around this restriction. Indeed, most malicious bots will report themselves as a common browser type, so that they appear innocuous in your log files. But this can also be done with plug-ins for most commonly used browsers.

It is possible to combine the two approaches, using environment variables as well as techniques from mod_rewrite, by using the %{ENV:variable} syntax, as follows:

```
SetEnvIf User-Agent evilbot go-away=1
<Directory /var/www>
    RewriteCond %{ENV:go-away} 1
    RewriteRule . - [F]
</Directory>
```

Problem: We Want to Prevent "Image Theft"

In this example, imagine that other websites are "stealing" our bandwidth by embedding our images in their pages, and we want to prevent that.

Solution

```
RewriteEngine On
RewriteCond %{HTTP_REFERER} !^www\.mysite\.com
RewriteCond %{HTTP_REFERER} !^$
RewriteRule \.(gif|jpg|png)$ - [F]
```

Discussion

The preceding rule set refuses requests for images if those images are not referred from this site. In other words, unless the images are embedded in pages from our site, we don't want anybody to see them.

This problem tends to arise most frequently when someone sees an image on your website, likes it, and embeds it directly in one of their web pages. This means that every time someone loads this page from their site, it generates requests to your site. They are, in a sense, stealing your bandwidth to serve their website.

What would be preferred would be if they saved a local copy of that image and then served that copy from their site. Or, of course, if they used their own images, rather than stealing your hard work for their site.

The first rewrite condition (%{HTTP_REFERER} !^www\.mysite\.com) checks to see that the image is referred from our site, which would be consistent with it being embedded in a page from our site, or at least linked from our site. Or, more accurately, it checks for requests that did not originate from our request, so that it will only run the RewriteRule in that case.

The second condition (%{HTTP_REFERER} !^$) ensures that we don't reject requests made directly for the image without a referer. We may or may not want to retain this condition, but it avoids requests from getting rejected unnecessarily when the browser, for whatever reason, simply doesn't return a referer. This can happen for a variety of reasons. Some browsers, for example, can be configured never to return referer information, for reasons of privacy. And a browser will not return a referer if someone gets to the page via a bookmark or by typing the URL directly into the browser address bar.

Finally, the RewriteRule itself matches any request for GIF, JPG, or PNG image files and returns a Forbidden response.

```
RewriteRule \.(gif|jpg|png)$ - [F]
```

The regular expression specifies that the filename end in .gif, .jpg, or .png to cover the major image types. The target of the rule is -, which indicates that no rewriting is to be done. But the flag, [F], indicates that a Forbidden status code is to be sent to the client.

Variants on this rule include rewriting the image request to something requesting that they load a file from their own site:

```
RewriteRule \.(gif|jpg|png)$ /var/www/images/please_dont_steal.gif
```

or redirecting the request to some other site:

```
RewriteRule \.(gif|jpg|png)$ http://other.site.com/images/unsavory.gif [R]
```

It's important to remember, when using this last approach, that you are merely redirecting the undesired activity directed against your site to some other site, which may be equally unappreciative of it. However, the most common result when you do this type of redirection is that the site that is using your image will immediately notice the change and stop attempting to use the remote image at all.

Summary

In conclusion, mod_rewrite really isn't the right way to do access control, most of the time. You should always consider the standard techniques, which are more reliable and faster, before resorting to mod_rewrite. One notable exception to this is time-based restrictions, as discussed in Chapter 5.

It's good to be aware of the [F] flag and the ways in which it can be used—just don't be too anxious to use it.

## CHAPTER 10

Virtual Hosts

Virtual hosts provide a way to run more than one website on the same physical server machine, on the same installation of Apache. Apache has provided this functionality since version 1.0.

There are two types of virtual hosts: *IP-based* virtual hosts, where each virtual host requires its own IP address, and *name-based* virtual hosts, where multiple virtual hosts can coexist on the same IP address by virtue of having different hostnames. In this chapter, we will concern ourselves exclusively with name-based virtual hosts. For a more thorough treatment of virtual hosts, you should consult the Apache virtual host documentation at `http://httpd.apache.org/docs/2.0/vhosts/`.

Creating a virtual host is a simple matter. However, when you need to create hundreds or thousands of virtual hosts, it becomes necessary to find a simpler way of managing them, since having hundreds of virtual host configuration blocks in your Apache configuration file becomes unmanageable. A number of techniques are available for dealing with this problem. mod_rewrite remains one of the most popular ways to solve this problem.

In this chapter, we'll briefly discuss the more conventional ways to create virtual hosts and look at mod_vhost_alias, a module specifically for mass virtual hosting. Then we'll talk about a variety of ways to create virtual hosts using mod_rewrite.

Virtual Hosts the Old-Fashioned Way

For this chapter, assume that you desire to run multiple websites on a single IP address. The websites will be distinguished by their names. So, if someone accesses `http://www.domain1.com/`, we want them to get their content out of /home/domain1/web. If they access `http://www.domain2.com/`, we want them to get content out of /home/domain2/web.

In order to configure this, you would add the following lines to your Apache configuration file:

```
NameVirtualHost *:80

<VirtualHost *:80>
        ServerName www.domain1.com
        ServerAlias domain1.com
        DocumentRoot /home/domain1/web
</VirtualHost>

<VirtualHost *:80>
        ServerName www.domain2.com
        ServerAlias domain2.dom
        DocumentRoot /home/domain2/web
</VirtualHost>
```

This creates two virtual hosts. Also, each host has an alternate name, or ServerAlias, without the www part of the hostname. That is, the first virtual host will respond to http:// www.domain1.com/ as well as to http://domain1.com/.

Creating virtual hosts does not cause the hostname to resolve to your IP address. You will also need to create DNS host entries so that the name resolves to your IP address, but this topic is beyond the scope of this book. If you don't know how to do this, you should consult your local network specialist or your ISP.

Unfortunately, once you have a few hundred of these virtual host configuration blocks, two problems start to appear. First, there's the human problem of actually managing all of these virtual host blocks in your configuration file. It's hard to find the one you want to edit. And when a problem occurs, it's often a huge hassle tracking it down across all of these configuration sections.

For small numbers of hosts (where the meaning of "small" depends on factors like your available time and patience), you may in fact solve this problem by using the Include configuration directive. For example, what I typically do is put each virtual host configuration in its own file named, for example, rcbowen.com.conf. These files are placed in a vhosts/ subdirectory of my main configuration directory. In the Apache configuration file, I put

```
Include conf/vhosts/*.conf
```

Every file in that directory with a .conf extension will be loaded and included in my server configuration. Note that the file path is relative to your ServerRoot configuration, so if you have your ServerRoot directive set to /usr/local/apache, then the file path will be /usr/local/apache/conf/vhosts/*.conf.

■**Note** You can also use the syntax `Include conf/vhosts/*`, which will include every file in the directory, removing the need to have special file names. However, this can also include files you hadn't intended, such as editor temporary files, and other things that happen to be in that directory.

Using per-vhost configuration files is good enough for most web servers. However, there are times when you want dynamically generated virtual host configurations. There are a variety of different reasons this might be needed. Perhaps you have a lot of customers. Or perhaps you are lazy. But most of the time, these motives can all be put under the same general heading. I want my web server to just do the right thing and not make me tell it every time. I don't want to have to change my configuration file just because I added a new virtual host. It is also worth noting that when the number of virtual hosts becomes large, the configuration consumes a large amount of memory, and server startup time is proportional to the number of virtual hosts you have.

You can dynamically configure virtual hosts with mod_rewrite, of course, but you can also do so with an Apache module called mod_vhost_alias, which I'll talk about first.

Configuring Virtual Hosts with mod_vhost_alias

The problem of mass virtual hosting has been around for quite a while. One of the earliest means of solving it was with mod_vhost_alias, which allows for dynamic configuration of virtual host document roots based on the hostname. While this module does somewhat limit what you can and cannot do with a virtual host, if you have a large number of hosts—all of which have exactly the same requirements—this module may be what you're looking for.

You can read up on all the details about mod_vhost_alias at http://httpd.apache.org/docs/2.0/mod/mod_vhost_alias.html, but we'll cover the basics here.

First, we need to decide on a common directory structure into which all of our virtual hosts will be placed. For example, we might decide that the content for a virtual host named www.example.com will be served out of a directory called /www/www.example.com/docs, and that the same pattern will apply for every one of our virtual hosts.

To do this with mod_rewrite, we can create a document root template, using the hostname as the name of the directory. mod_vhost_alias puts the name of the requested virtual host in a variable called %0, which can be used to specify the template to be used for all virtual host document roots:

```
VirtualDocumentRoot /www/%0/docs
```

If, on the other hand, we want to just use a portion of the hostname, such as the example of `www.example.com`, we need to use a slightly different approach. To accomplish this, we need to think of the hostname for the virtual host in three parts. Part one, which we'll call `%1`, is `www`. Part two, which we'll call `%2`, is `example`. And part three, which we'll call `%3`, is `com`.

Keeping those names in mind, you can now configure all of your virtual hosts with a single configuration directive:

```
VirtualDocumentRoot /www/%2/docs
```

This will map every virtual host the right place, based on its hostname.

Of course, we'll have to make sure that directory exists, and we'll have to make sure that the hostname does in fact resolve to the IP address of our Apache server. But, we won't ever have to change our configuration file or restart our Apache server in order to add a new virtual host.

There are a number of issues that you'll start thinking about shortly after you first implement this technique of mass virtual hosting, if you haven't already started considering them. Some of these I'll address right away in the sections that follow, and others I'll leave for later in the chapter.

www.example.com works, but example.com Doesn't

The technique just described requires that the hostname be in three parts and that the directory be named after the second part. Thus, `www.example.com` maps to `/www/example/docs`, and `www.boxofclue.com` maps to `/www/boxofclue/docs`, but `example.com` and `boxofclue.com` both map to `/www/com/docs`, which is distinctly not what we wanted to happen. Fortunately, there is a very simple solution to this: just look at the hostname backward.

This time, instead of looking at `www.example.com` as parts one, two, and three, we'll look at it the other way around. We'll call `com` part number –1, `example` part number –2, and `www` part number –3. With this approach, the `www` part becomes completely optional, and we can configure our virtual hosts as follows:

```
VirtualDocumentRoot /www/%-2/docs
```

So why didn't I just tell you that to begin with? Well, some people find the other explanation is somewhat easier to understand, so it makes sense to start there. But when you can count from the right or the left, it allows you to handle hostnames whichever way makes the most sense to you.

An alternative approach is to create symbolic links for all the various possible aliases for a given virtual host. So, for example, `/www/example.com/docs` might in fact be a symbolic link to `/www/www.example.com/docs`, so that both hostnames point to the same content.

There Are Too Many Directories

This problem tends to happen only at large ISPs. If you're not one of those, you may not care much about this scenario, and you can probably skip this section.

If you have hundreds—or even thousands—of virtual hosts, you'll encounter the situation where the directories are just too many to manage. For example, say the /www directory contains several thousand subdirectories, and it's just getting too much to manage. You want to subdivide a little further. You may want to separate the subdirectories into one directory per letter. Or, for the really huge ISPs, perhaps you want to subdivide even further.

mod_vhost_alias allows you to consider not only distinct parts of the hostname, but also the individual letters of each part. So, if you want to divide into one directory per letter, you can consider the first letter of the second part. That is, if you want to put www.example.com into the directory /www/e/example/docs, then you need to look for the first letter of part number 2. You would call this first letter %2.1, the second letter would be %2.2, and so on. If you want the second letter and everything following it (xample in this case), then you would call that %2.2+.

So, for one directory per letter, you use this:

```
VirtualDocumentRoot /www/%2.1/%2/%2/docs
```

For further subdivision, you might use this:

```
VirtualDocumentRoot /www/%2.1/%2.2/%2/docs
```

The first of these two examples will give you a directory, /www/e/example/docs, in which to put www.example.com, whereas with the second example, you'll need to put it in /www/e/x/example/docs.

The variations on this are, of course, without end, depending on the number of virtual hosts you have and the amount of complexity you can put up with. You could also, for example, have a different directory for each hostname within a particular domain (which some people will refer to as *subdomains*[1]), and this can be accomplished with the following:

```
VirtualDocumentRoot /www/%-3/%-2/docs
```

Or perhaps you could subdivide by top-level domain (the .com or .org bit):

```
VirtualDocumentRoot /www/%-1/%-2/docs
```

You should pick a directory structure that is easy to understand and well documented, but, beyond that, the choice is entirely up to you.

---

1. Incorrectly, in my opinion.

This Approach Breaks My Other Virtual Hosts

Yes, unfortunately, the biggest pitfall with this approach is that it breaks your other virtual hosts. You need to pick one approach or the other. If you use mod_vhost_alias alongside traditional `<VirtualHost>` configuration blocks, you are almost certain to run into problems.

It's the "almost certain" part that tends to be more than a little confusing. You'll encounter some people who will assert most vociferously that "It works for me!" and they tend to greatly confuse the issue. There are indeed certain circumstances in which mod_vhost_alias and regular virtual hosts can happily coexist. However, virtual hosts in the same configuration as mod_vhost_alias do tend to be very fragile, and the smallest misconfiguration can cause them to do not only incorrect, but sometimes completely unpredictable things. So, as much as you or someone else wants to assert that it worked for you once and should work for you again, I strongly encourage you to avoid using mod_vhost_alias in conjunction with other virtual hosting techniques. It will very likely break things.

Logging

I'll discuss logging a little later, but it's worth at least mentioning here, as it is a common complaint about mod_vhost_alias. All of the virtual hosts log to a single log file. You'll have to either put up with that or use one of the techniques described in the "Logging for Mass Virtual Hosts" section later in this chapter.

It's Too Inflexible

Eventually, you'll run up against the fact that mod_vhost_alias is just very inflexible. It does not permit per-vhost changes. So, if one of your virtual hosts needs a particular change to it, there's no easy way to do it.

The most common solution to this is to allow the various virtual hosts to modify their configuration using `.htaccess` files. You can also modify their configuration using `<Directory>` blocks in the main configuration file, but, since the goal was to avoid having to change the configuration file at all, this is usually undesirable.

Mass Virtual Hosting with mod_rewrite

This brings us to the heart of this chapter. Since this is, after all, a book about mod_rewrite, it's about time we got around to talking about it.

Handling mass virtual hosting (or even just a small number of virtual hosts) is, after beautifying ugly URLs, the most popular use of mod_rewrite. Fortunately, it's fairly easy and well documented.

There are a number of different ways we might go about handling virtual hosts. We're going to look at two solutions, each of which approaches the problem slightly differently.

Rewriting Virtual Hosts

We'll start with the most common approach, which is to do a simple rewrite to a file path, based on the value of the SERVER_NAME header. This gives us a rule set like this:

```
RewriteEngine On

RewriteMap lowercase int:tolower
RewriteRule ^/(.*)$ /www/${lowercase:%{SERVER_NAME}}/docs/$1
```

Using this rule set, a request for documents from www.example.com is mapped to the directory /www/www.example.com/docs/. This is almost the same directory that we created with the mod_vhost_alias configuration, except that the entire hostname is used.

The RewriteMap is necessary because the hostname might be uppercase or lowercase, and we need to make sure that we have only one possible target file path for each request. Using the internal rewrite map function tolower, we lowercase the requested hostname and rewrite to a file path created using that hostname.

This approach, as shown here, immediately creates a couple of problems. We'll tackle the easier ones first.

www.example.com works, but example.com Doesn't

As with mod_vhost_alias, we have the problem where requests for www.example.com will be handled correctly, while requests for example.com will generate File Not Found errors. We want those two hostnames to be treated the same, and this requires a little more work. Since mod_rewrite doesn't have an immediate way to pull off the different parts of the hostname, we need to do this using RewriteCond.

Our modified rule set looks like the following:

```
RewriteEngine On

RewriteMap lowercase int:tolower
RewriteCond %{HTTP_HOST} ^(www\.)?(.*)$
RewriteRule ^/(.*)$ /www/${lowercase:%2}/docs/$1
```

The RewriteCond directive doesn't really act as a conditional here, but serves only to pull out the component parts of the hostname. The leading www. on the hostname becomes optional, and the rest of the hostname is used to generate the file path.

Now, requests for both www.example.com and example.com are mapped to the directory /www/hosts/example.com/docs.

There Are Too Many Directories

As with mod_vhost_alias, we'll quickly create a large number of subdirectories in the /www/ directory. Fortunately, mod_rewrite makes it almost as easy to pull off the first letter and create per-letter subdirectories.

So, the next iteration of our rule looks like this:

```
RewriteEngine On

RewriteMap lowercase int:tolower
RewriteCond %{HTTP_HOST} ^(www\.)?(.)(.*)$
RewriteRule ^/(.*)$ /www/${lowercase:%2}/${lowercase:%3}/docs/$1
```

The regular expression this time pulls off the (optional) leading www. part and then matches a single character, followed by the rest of the string. These various parts are then available to be used in the rewrite rule, and we end up with a request for www.example.com (or example.com) being served out of the directory /www/e/xample.com/docs/. You'll notice that this is slightly different from the directory path we ended up with when using mod_vhost_alias.

■**Note** Remember that when using .htaccess files, you will need to remove the leading slash from the RewriteRule. Although it is extremely unlikely that you will be rewriting virtual hosts in an .htaccess file, it is, of course, possible. In this case, you'd change the RewriteRule to

```
RewriteRule ^(.*)$ /www/${lowercase:%2}/${lowercase:%3}/docs/$1
```

The earlier RewriteRule directives would also be adjusted in similar manner.

All My Aliases Quit Working

Because directives from mod_rewrite get run before those from mod_alias, Alias directives within a dynamically configured virtual host are not honored, and any documents that were to be served via an Alias will end up being requested out of the mapped virtual host directory instead.

In order to make those Alias directives continue to work, we need to make sure that the RewriteRule ignores them when it comes to rewriting the URIs to file paths. This is done with RewriteCond directives placed before the RewriteRules:

```
RewriteEngine On

RewriteMap lowercase int:tolower

# Skip the /icons/ alias
RewriteCond %{REQUEST_URI} !^/icons/

RewriteCond %{HTTP_HOST} ^(www\.)?(.*)$
RewriteRule ^/(.*)$ /www/${lowercase:%2}/docs/$1
```

With these URIs excluded from the RewriteRule, they can now be handled by the
Alias directive, when the time comes. However, this does result in a shared /icons
directory for all of your virtual hosts, which may not be what you had in mind.

CGI and Scripts Are Served As Plain Text

The rules developed so far work great for static files, since we are mapping requests to
file paths. However, for files that need to be treated specially, such as a CGI program,
this approach doesn't work very well. Specifically, you'll receive the file unprocessed;
that is, you'll receive the plain text unexecuted source code of the CGI program. This
is clearly a very bad thing, and we need to make sure it doesn't happen.

Fortunately, there is at least one fairly simple solution to this problem. We treat CGI
programs slightly differently:

```
RewriteEngine On
RewriteMap lowercase int:tolower

# Skip the global /icons/ alias
RewriteCond %{REQUEST_URI} !^/icons/

RewriteCond %{HTTP_HOST} ^(www\.)?(.*)$
RewriteRule ^/cgi-bin/(.*) /${lowercase:%2}/cgi-bin/$2 [PT,L]
RewriteRule ^/(.*)$ /www/${lowercase:%2}/docs/$1

ScriptAliasMatch ^/([^/]+)/cgi-bin/(.*) /www/$1/cgi-bin/$2
```

This rule set assumes that each virtual host directory contains a cgi-bin/ subdirectory, as well as the docs/ subdirectory that we've been putting our documents into.
Requests for CGI programs are mapped into the directory via a two-step process.

First, any URL starting with /cgi-bin/ is rewritten to /hostname/cgi-bin/ instead.
Second, any request that starts with /something/cgi-bin is mapped to

/www/something/cgi-bin with the `ScriptAliasMatch` directive, which also ensures that all files in this directory are executed as CGI programs. Thus, each dynamically created virtual host now has its own CGI directory.

In this last version of the rule set, we're able to handle any number of virtual hosts, each with its own CGI directory. And we're also correctly handling /icons/ or any other global `Alias` directives that we'd like to continue working.

Virtual Hosts with RewriteMap

There remains one alternate approach we might take to create dynamic virtual hosts that is well worth discussing.

The techniques that we've looked at so far will allow any hostname to be mapped to a directory. That is, any hostname that resolves to your IP address will be mapped to some directory. This isn't necessarily always what you want.

For example, there may be names that resolve to your address that you don't really want to map to a website at all, either because you want them to go somewhere else or perhaps because they are names that someone has mistakenly (or without your permission) pointed at your address. Or maybe your directory structure doesn't in fact abide by a well-defined rule, and different names map to directories that are not easily determined from just the hostname.

In either of these cases, `RewriteMap` might provide a better solution. Having a `RewriteMap` that explicitly maps hostnames to directory paths will ensure that only hostnames you want to support are supported, and it will also ensure that each hostname goes to the right place, even if it doesn't match a particular pattern.

The first step is to create a map file, listing all of our approved hostnames and the directory path to which they should map. This file will look like this:

```
www.example1.com /home/example1/www
example1.com /home/example1/www
www.example2.com /var/www/vhosts/example2
www.example4.com /export/home/joeuser/public_html
www.example3.com /www/example3
```

When we're done, this will map these hosts—and only these hosts—to particular directories. It's important to remember that if something is not on the list, it won't get mapped. So the hostname example2.com (without the www) will not be mapped to the directory /var/www/hosts/example2 as you might expect, because it doesn't appear on the list.

Once we've created the map file, we need to use it in our configuration file. As before, this rule set assumes that each virtual host directory contains a docs subdirectory, as well as a cgi-bin subdirectory, which will contain static documents and CGI programs, respectively. Assuming that we named the map file vhosts.map, we would add the following configuration lines to the configuration file:

```
RewriteEngine On

# Uppercase or lowercase
RewriteMap lowercase int:tolower

# Virtual hosts map
RewriteMap vhost txt:/www/conf/vhosts.map

# Exclude the global aliases, if desired
RewriteCond %{REQUEST_URI} !^/icons/

# Rewrite cgi requests
RewriteRule ^/cgi-bin/(.*) \
    /${vhost:%{${lowercase:%HTTP_HOST}}|/www/mainhost}/cgi-bin/$1 [PT,L]
ScriptAliasMatch /(.*?)/cgi-bin/(.*) /$1/cgi-bin/$2

# Then, everything else
RewriteCond ^/(.*)$ ${vhost:%{${lowercase:%HTTP_HOST}}|/www/mainhost}/docs/$1
```

This rule set assumes that each virtual host directory contains a /docs/ subdirectory for the documents and a /cgi-bin/ directory for the CGI programs, if any. Other than that, the virtual hosts can be located anywhere at all in the file system for this technique to work.

I mentioned at the beginning of this section that hostnames that do not explicitly appear in the map file won't get mapped to the desired directory, but will end up being mapped to the default content directory. In the case of the rule set just shown, that directory will be /www/mainhost, or whatever you changed it to.

Logging for Mass Virtual Hosts

Finally, we'll address the question that we've been putting off since early on in the chapter. When we move to mass virtual hosting, rather than having a separate <VirtualHost> block for each virtual host, it becomes more difficult to have individual log files for each vhost.

There are a few different ways to solve this problem. Which one is the best solution for you is, of course, up to you. But here are some suggestions.

Splitting the Log File

The easiest solution for logging multiple virtual hosts is to stick to a single log file and then split it up afterward. The disadvantage of this approach is that live log files contain entries from all of the virtual hosts and are therefore less useful than they could be.

Two things are necessary for this approach. First, we need to add an additional field to our log directive:

```
UseCanonicalName Off
LogFormat "%V %h %l %u %t \"%r\" %s %b" vcommon
CustomLog logs/access_log vcommon
```

This adds to the beginning of every log file entry an additional field, which is the name of virtual host requested. In this way, every line in the log file is clearly associated with the virtual host to which it is attached. This also allows us to split the log file out into its component parts later on.

The `UseCanonicalName Off` directive is important in that it disables Apache's default behavior of using the canonical hostname—that is, the one that is set in the `ServerName` directive, in the main configuration file, when referring to the server's hostname. The `%V` variable in the preceding `LogFormat` directive will then be set to the hostname that the user typed into their browser. The variable `%v` (lowercase v, as opposed to uppercase V), on the other hand, will be set to the canonical hostname. In the case of dynamically generated virtual hosts, that would cause all log entries to have the same hostname— that is, whatever was set in the main `ServerName` directive.

The second step is to split up the file into its component parts. This is done with the `split-logfile` script, which comes with Apache. If you have installed Apache from source, this script will be located in the `support/` directory of the source distribution. Unfortunately, if you have installed Apache from a third-party package, this file might not have been installed at all. You will need to look around. The complete documentation for this script is located at `http://httpd.apache.org/docs/2.0/programs/other.html`, but there is very little to it. The script is used by running it with the log file as input, and it creates one file per virtual host in the directory where you are running the script.

```
split-logfile < access_log
```

Each of the generated files will be named with the name of the virtual host.

Using Piped Log Handlers

The disadvantage of using `split-logfile` to handle your logs is that the logs are not available per-virtual host until later. Usually, you will run the `split-logfile` script periodically, perhaps via a `cron` job. But at the exact moment that you need the log files for the purpose of troubleshooting, they will all still be in the single monolithic log file, making it difficult to pick out the log file entries that you are looking for. This problem can be at least partially solved by using a piped log file handler, but there is one very large caveat.

When you are doing dynamic virtual hosts, having just a single log file ensures that you will not use up a huge number of file descriptors. If you use piped log file handlers to create a single log file for each virtual host, you will start to use up large numbers of file descriptors and run the risk of using up all available file descriptors, thus causing your server to die. It is therefore very important that, as the number of virtual hosts grows, you keep an eye on the number of available file descriptors and stop before it's too late.

Having said that, it is possible to use a slightly modified version of the `split-logfile` script to have a piped log file handler with a single log file for each virtual host.

Since `split-logfile` expects input on STDIN, it seems like it should be ideal for use as a piped log file handler. Unfortunately, it creates the log files in the directory in which it is run, whereas when you are using a piped log file handler you want to make sure that you can control exactly where it puts the output.

Summary

With one or more of the techniques described in this chapter, you are able to create dynamic virtual hosts for your web server. However, it's important to remember that virtual hosts are fragile. Combining several methods of creating virtual hosts, such as rewrite rules and traditional virtual host blocks, or perhaps mod_vhost_alias, can produce unexpected interaction and unpredictable results. It may indeed work the way you expect, but then again, it might not. For best results, you should pick one technique and stick with it. This will lead to scenarios that are easier to troubleshoot and fix when things go wrong.

CHAPTER 11

■ ■ ■

Proxying

If mod_proxy is installed, mod_rewrite can be used to force requests through the proxy mechanism to another server, or perhaps to another part of the same server. This technique is used for a wide variety of purposes, such as load balancing and server migration. In this chapter, I'll cover the syntax involved in rewriting to a proxy and discuss the various intricacies of this technique.

Apache comes with several modules that allow you to run a proxy server. With Apache 1.3, the caching and proxying functions are combined in mod_proxy. In 2.0, these functions are split into several submodules. And in 2.2, the proxying functionality was overhauled to provide a variety of load balancing functions as well.

mod_proxy gives you the [P] flag so that you have access to all of this functionality via the rewrite engine, allowing you to map URLs arbitrarily through the proxying mechanism.

Proxy Rewrite Rules

A RewriteRule is a proxy rule if it has a [P] flag appended to it. This causes mod_rewrite to make a subrequest via the proxy mechanism to the target URL. mod_proxy must be installed for this to work correctly. In Apache 2.x you'll also need mod_proxy_http, or, if you're wanting to proxy FTP addresses, mod_proxy_ftp.

```
RewriteRule ^/images/(.*) http://images.example.com/$1 [P]
```

The example given here causes a transparent proxying of the request to another server, which will serve the images. That is to say, the browser user is not aware that the change has occurred.

In the spirit of learning when not to use mod_rewrite, I should note that this example could have been accomplished using ProxyPass instead:

```
ProxyPass /images/ http://images.example.com/
```

There are a number of scenarios where proxying is useful, but they all come down to one thing: the content being requested is, in fact, on some other server. The reasons for it being on another server are varied, of course.

Security

Whenever mod_proxy is enabled, it is important to take a moment to discuss security. A misconfigured proxy server can be used by malicious people for a variety of attacks, but it's fairly simple to avoid this situation.

Using mod_proxy outbound requests is called *forward proxying*. Forward proxying describes a situation where browsers on your LAN have this server configured as their proxy server for all outbound web requests. This is how proxying was initially used most commonly. The reasons for forward proxying are primarily performance and control.

If all outbound requests are funneled through a proxy server, this gives an easy way for someone to control what websites users are going to, via some kind of filtering mechanism placed on that proxy server. And if the proxy server is also able to cache requested content, this increases the perceived speed of web traffic, since commonly requested documents can be retrieved from the cache, rather than having to connect to the actual website to retrieve the document.

Reverse proxying, on the other hand, is the term used for the situation more akin to what we want to do with mod_rewrite. That is, an inbound connection, from the outside internet to your web server, is proxied to one or more back-end servers.

The risk occurs when a proxy server is configured to be an *open forward proxy*. This term means that anyone can proxy anything they like through the proxy server. Thus, users can use an open proxy server to circumvent corporate content filtering restrictions, such as visiting pornographic websites via your proxy server, thereby hiding this activity from their network administrators. Or, web-based attacks can be launched at a website through your proxy server, so that those attacks appear to come from your network, rather than from that of the real attacker. Also, since the CONNECT method can be used for any protocol—not just HTTP—it is very common to proxy spam and other email through misconfigured proxy servers.

These kinds of exploits have the dual effect of filling your network connection with other folks' traffic and making it appear that traffic is coming from you, thus possibly making you partially liable for malicious or even illegal activities. So, before we go any further in this chapter, I want to point you to some basic security tips for setting up a secure proxy server. This is even more important when using mod_rewrite to do the proxying, simply because when people use mod_rewrite to do proxying, they tend not to think of it as a proxy server, but merely some rewrite rules.

Fortunately, for most scenarios, the solution is very simple. Forbid forward proxying, and the problem goes away. This is accomplished with the ProxyRequests directive:

```
ProxyRequests Off
```

This forbids any proxying, except to hosts that are explicitly listed in ProxyPass directives and RewriteRule directives. This is the best possible scenario.

If, on the other hand, you are actually setting up a forward proxy server and happen also to be using it for reverse proxying, another solution is necessary. The syntax for this will differ slightly depending on whether you are running Apache 1.3 or 2.0.

Apache 1.3

In Apache 1.3, you would need something like the following:

```
<Directory proxy:*>
      Order deny,allow
      Deny from all
      Allow from 192.168.0
      Allow from 127.0.0.1
</Directory>
```

This configuration block, placed in your main server configuration file, will forbid anyone from using the proxy server other than people on your local network or the machine itself. You will, of course, have to replace 192.168.0 with the subnet that you are using on your particular network.

Proxy requests made explicitly via a ProxyPass directive or with a RewriteRule with a [P] flag will be able to get through, because the request will be seen as coming from 127.0.0.1, the IP address of the loopback address on the server itself.

Apache 2.0

In Apache 2.0, a new syntax is available for this sort of thing, so that the less intuitive <Directory> syntax needn't be used:

```
<Proxy *>
      Order deny,allow
      Deny from all
      Allow from 192.168.0
      Allow from 127.0.0.1
</Proxy>
```

This configuration block has the exact effect of the 1.3 block shown earlier, but the syntax is a little more intuitive. Proxy requests are permitted from the local network and from the machine itself. This protects you from unknown clients proxying content through your server.

Proxying Without mod_rewrite

As usual, an in-depth knowledge of mod_rewrite includes knowing when not to use it. Although this section doesn't present a complete discussion of mod_proxy, it's important to know that your most common proxying needs can be fulfilled without the use of mod_rewrite.

If you wanted, for example, to proxy a single directory to another server, you should do this with the `ProxyPass` directive, rather than with mod_rewrite:

```
ProxyPass /images/ http://images.example.com/images/
ProxyPassReverse /images/ http://images.example.com/images/
```

This creates a proxy through this server to another server called `images.example.com`, but only for requests in the `/images/` directory. Thus, a request for the URL `http://www.example.com/images/monkey.jpg` will in fact be satisfied by making a request for the URI `http://images.example.com/images/monkey.jpg`, and then returned as though it came instead from `www.example.com`.

The `ProxyPassReverse` directive ensures that any response headers containing the `images.example.com` hostname will be rewritten to the `www.example.com` hostname instead, so that the browser never becomes aware of the `images.example.com` hostname at all. This is very important because without it you could run into a situation where a browser is receiving redirect headers for a machine that is not in fact reachable at all.

It is important also to understand that any absolute URL references embedded in proxied HTML pages will not be rewritten. Thus, proxied HTML pages need to contain relative URLs, or the browser will be unable to reach the linked content.

A module called mod_proxy_html exists to solve this problem, but a full treatment of it is beyond the scope of this book. You can find a very good write-up of this module, as well as other proxying techniques, at `http://www.apacheweek.com/features/reverseproxies`.

If an entire virtual host is to be proxied to another server, the syntax would look very similar to that presented earlier:

```
ProxyPass / http://other.example.com/
ProxyPassReverse / http://other.example.com/
```

Placing these rules inside a virtual host or in the main server configuration file will cause that entire host to be served from the other server, via the proxy mechanism.

Once you start doing this kind of global proxying, the most common question to come up is how you can exclude certain things from this proxying. That's where mod_rewrite comes in.

Proxying with mod_rewrite

mod_rewrite should be used for proxying when the structure of the content to be proxied is more complex than simply a directory or an entire virtual host. If a regular expression pattern can be written to describe the content to be proxied, then mod_rewrite may be the right solution to the problem.

I'll start with a few examples that exactly mirror the examples given in the earlier non-mod_rewrite section. First, here's a RewriteRule that causes proxying of the /images/ directory on a front-end server:

```
RewriteEngine On
RewriteRule ^/images/(.*) http://images.example.com/images/$1 [P]
ProxyPassReverse /images/ http://images.example.com/images/
```

The ProxyPassReverse directive is still needed, for exactly the reasons cited before. The [P] rewrite directive is passed off to mod_proxy, and so everything from that point is exactly the same as if you had used a ProxyPass directive.

To mimic the previous "proxy everything" configuration, we'd alter the rewrite rule set in the expected way:

```
RewriteEngine On
RewriteRule (.*) http://other.example.com$1 [P]
ProxyPassReverse / http://other.example.com
```

However, neither of these rule sets are particularly useful, since, in each case, we should have used ProxyPass instead. Now let's consider a task where mod_rewrite is much more useful.

Proxying a Particular File Type

In the first real example, imagine that we're trying to reduce the load on our web server by offloading some of the content to a back-end server. As before, the images directory will be moved to another server. Unfortunately, images are scattered throughout the entire server directory structure, rather than all being conveniently located in one place.

Rather than trying to hunt down all of the images on the entire server, we'll just copy the entire document directory to the back-end image server, and then we'll just proxy any request that looks like an image. Over time, perhaps we can consolidate all of the images in a single directory, but for now, we'll leave the structure as it is.

```
RewriteEngine On
RewriteRule (.*\.(jpg|gif|png)) http://images.example.com$1 [P]
ProxyPassReverse / http://images.example.com/
```

In this case, the `ProxyPassReverse` really isn't necessary, since every request passed to the back-end server will be a fully qualified request for a particular image file. However, since it's a good habit to be in, and doesn't hurt anything, let's leave that in there.

Any request for a file ending in `jpg`, `gif`, or `png` will be proxied to the back-end image server, and, since the directory trees match, the image will be there. As more image files are added to the server, a more logical structure for image placement may be followed, eventually removing the need for this much complexity.

Proxying to an Application Server

When you're running Apache as an application server, you may find that this causes a significant performance degradation. mod_proxy may be used to improve this situation by segregating your static and dynamic content to different servers. The static content can be served very quickly, while the dynamic requests are proxied to a back-end server that runs only that content.

A fairly common configuration for this is to run that secondary server on the same physical machine, but on another port. Consider, for example, a site powered by mod_perl. The static content is served from the front-end server, but the mod_perl content is served by another server process dedicated to that purpose, running on a high port. It is configured to just run a few child processes, so that mod_perl's rather large memory requirements don't drag down the performance of the front-end static content server.

Say, for example, that we are running the mod_perl server on port 8888. We then want to map all requests for content in the `/cgi-perl/` URL-space, as well as any request for a PL file, to the back-end mod_perl server:

```
RewriteEngine On
RewriteRule ^/cgi-perl/(.*) http://localhost:8888/cgi-perl/$1 [P]
RewriteRule (.*)\.pl$ http://localhost:8888$1.pl [P]
ProxyPassReverse / http://localhost:8888/
```

This same technique (and variations on it) can also be used for other application servers, such as Plone, Tomcat, or even content running from an IIS server. In Apache 2.2, the new module mod_proxy_ajp is specifically for proxying to Tomcat and other application servers that speak the Apache JServ protocol.

Modifying Proxied Content

The documentation for mod_ext_filter (`http://httpd.apache.org/docs/2.0/mod/mod_ext_filter.html`) demonstrates how to pass content through an external filter such as `gzip`. Using this technique, along with a proxy, you can fetch remote content and modify it slightly before passing it on to the end user.

In the following example, we can provide a way to translate the contents of another website into another language or dialect, by passing them through our proxy server. Rather than implementing a full language translation gateway, this example merely provides the contents of a website in "Swedish Chef"[1] dialect. Adapting this to translate into Swahili or ancient Greek is left as an exercise for the reader.

To use this example, you will need to obtain and install the GNU Talk Filters, which you may obtain from `http://www.hyperrealm.com/main.php?s=talkfilters`. There are a variety of other filters also available in this package.

Next, add the following configuration to your Apache configuration file:

```
ExtFilterDefine chef mode=output cmd=/usr/local/bin/chef
RewriteEngine On
RewriteRule ^/swedish/([^/]+)/(.*) http://$1/$2 [P]
<Location /swedish>
    SetOutputFilter chef
</Location>
```

This configuration will cause URLs of the form `http://www.yoursite.com/swedish/ www.otherhost.com/index.html` to serve up the contents of `http://www.otherhost.com/ index.html` through the filter, thus translating everything to Swedish Chef.

While this is good for a laugh, there are rather serious problems involved in using this for a real site. In particular, you'll find that most links from within pages don't go to the expected places. If you wanted to use this technique for more than just amusement, you might want to look at mod_proxy_html (`http://apache.webthing.com/mod_proxy_html/`), which will also fix these links as they get passed through the proxy.

Excluding Content from the Proxy

I was recently in a position of migrating a website to Apache from another web server software. At the same time, design changes were being made, and much of the code was being moved to PHP from another language.

It was decided that the best way to proceed was to put Apache on a new server and proxy all requests through to the old server. Then, as content was moved, or new parts of the website were put on the new server, those portions of the website would no longer be proxied. This started out simply enough, with a rewrite rule and a few exclusions:

```
RewriteEngine On
RewriteCond %{REQUEST_URI} !^/(admissions|alumni|athletics)/ [NC]
RewriteRule (.*) http://oldwww.example.edu$1 [P]
ProxyPassReverse / http://oldwww.example.edu/
```

---

1. The Swedish Chef, for those that don't know, was a character on *The Muppet Show* television program. This character had a rather distinctive accent and dialect. See `http://en.wikipedia.org/wiki/ Swedish_Chef` for more details.

Every URL that didn't start with `admissions`, `alumni`, or `athletics` would be prox-ied through to the old server. This let us transparently migrate content to the new server and still keep all the existing content working until such time as we could get around to fixing it.

So far so good. However, the list of exclusions grew with every week, and this very quickly got out of hand. We needed to come up with a more flexible solution that didn't require that the server configuration be changed every time something new was added to the server.

Looking Somewhere Else

The next solution that we came up with was much simpler. In words, it goes something like this. If the content is on the server, then serve it. If it's not, then proxy the request to the old server. This will also probably require some exclusions, but it should be more flexible and require fewer changes to the server configuration.

```
RewriteEngine On
# Is the requested resource here?
RewriteCond %{REQUEST_FILENAME} !-f
RewriteCond %{REQUEST_FILENAME} !-d
# If not …
RewriteRule (.*) http://oldwww.example.edu$1 [P]
ProxyPassReverse / http://oldwww.example.edu/
```

This same technique can be used in a nonproxy environment to look in several places for a requested file:

```
RewriteEngine On
# If it's not here …
RewriteCond %{REQUEST_URI} ^/images
RewriteCond %{REQUEST_FILENAME} !-f
# Look there instead …
RewriteRule ^/images/(.*) /pics/$1 [PT]
```

This technique is particularly useful if you are merging several different websites into one, or perhaps changing your directory structure policies to a new layout, and you want the migration period to be relatively painless.

Summary

There is much, much more you can do with mod_proxy and its related modules that is beyond the scope of this book. You can find the full documentation for mod_proxy at `http://httpd.apache.org/docs/2.0/mod/mod_proxy.html` or, if you're using Apache 1.3, at `http://httpd.apache.org/docs/1.3/mod/mod_proxy.html`.

CHAPTER 12

■ ■ ■

Debugging

This final chapter discusses the rewrite log, as well as other methods for debugging your rewrite rules and regular expressions. The rewrite log can also be good for optimizing these rules, by figuring out how they are actually being evaluated.

Many of the techniques discussed in this chapter assume that you are the administrator on your own server, or that you at least have a shell account and access to basic command-line tools. If this is not the case, then it will be in your best interest to install Apache on your desktop system and do this troubleshooting locally before moving content and rewrite rule sets up to your server. Of course, experimentation on a test server, rather than on the production server, is a good idea in any case.

RewriteLog

Your most important tool in debugging your rewrite rules is the RewriteLog directive. With the RewriteLog enabled, everything mod_rewrite does, or even attempts to do, is logged in great detail. It's a little cryptic, but it's great for stepping through exactly what went wrong.

To enable the RewriteLog, two directives are required:

```
RewriteLog logs/rewrite_log
RewriteLogLevel 9
```

The first of these two directives defines where the log file will be placed.

RewriteLogLevel should be set to a value between 1 and 9. The least verbose of these values is 1, and 9 is the most verbose. For the purposes of troubleshooting, you should have this value set to a higher rather than a lower number. However, be aware that this produces enormous quantities of log messages very quickly and should not be enabled on a production server. Set at its highest level, the RewriteLog grows at a rate of between 3 and 10—or even more—lines per request to the server, as you'll see in some of the upcoming examples.

The RewriteLog and RewriteLogLevel directives are not permitted in .htaccess files, and they must be set in the main server configuration file.

A Simple RewriteLog Example

The best way to see what sorts of things to expect in the RewriteLog and how to read them is to show an example of a rewriting happening.

The rule set that I tested with is as follows:

```
RewriteLog /www/logs/rewrite_log
RewriteLogLevel 9

RewriteEngine On
RewriteRule ^/one /www/htdocs/two.html
```

This is a simple redirect. mod_rewrite will need to examine the incoming request, determine whether it matches the pattern, and, if it does, rewrite the request to the target file path.

When I request the URL http://localhost/one, here's what gets logged in the RewriteLog:

```
127.0.0.1 - - [25/Oct/2005:10:52:30 --0400]
[localhost/sid#188df98][rid#18cb650/initial] (2) init rewrite engine with
requested uri /one
127.0.0.1 - - [25/Oct/2005:10:52:30 --0400]
[localhost/sid#188df98][rid#18cb650/initial] (3) applying pattern '^/one'
to uri '/one'
127.0.0.1 - - [25/Oct/2005:10:52:30 --0400]
[localhost/sid#188df98][rid#18cb650/initial] (2) rewrite /one ->
/usr/local/apache/htdocs/two.html
127.0.0.1 - - [25/Oct/2005:10:52:30 --0400]
[localhost/sid#188df98][rid#18cb650/initial] (2) local path result:
/usr/local/apache/htdocs/two.html
127.0.0.1 - - [25/Oct/2005:10:52:30 --0400]
[localhost/sid#188df98][rid#18cb650/initial] (1) go-ahead with
/usr/local/apache/htdocs/two.html [OK]
127.0.0.1 - - [25/Oct/2005:10:52:30 --0400]
[localhost/sid#188df98][rid#18d1650/initial] (2) init rewrite engine with
requested uri /favicon.ico
127.0.0.1 - - [25/Oct/2005:10:52:30 --0400]
[localhost/sid#188df98][rid#18d1650/initial] (3) applying pattern '^/one'
to uri '/favicon.ico'
127.0.0.1 - - [25/Oct/2005:10:52:30 --0400]
[localhost/sid#188df98][rid#18d1650/initial] (1) pass through /favicon.ico
```

First, a word about the format of the log entry. The first four fields are the same as the first fields in the access log. First, there's the IP address of the remote (client) host. Next, we have a field that is almost always blank, the remote ident of the client. The third field is the username of the remote user, if they had to authenticate to fetch this resource. And fourth is the current time and date, including the time zone offset.

The next two sets of square brackets, [localhost/sid#188df98][rid#18d1650/initial], are not particularly useful for the purposes of troubleshooting rewrite rules. It may be possible that these pieces of information may be useful in troubleshooting something at the level of the Apache C code, but, for the purposes of using mod_rewrite, they should probably be ignored. The two possibly useful pieces of information in there are the first and last strings. The first string indicates the virtual host to which the request was made. The initial indicates that the request was an initial request, as opposed to a subrequest.

For the record, the sid is the server ID, unique per virtual host, and the rid is the request ID, which may or may not be unique per request, depending on various circumstances that I won't go into here.

The part of the log entry that you really should be looking at starts with the number in parentheses. For the sake of readability, that's going to be the part of the log entries that I talk about for the rest of this chapter.

Here's that log sequence again, but with material removed that isn't actually very useful:

```
(2) init rewrite engine with requested uri /one
(3) applying pattern '^/one' to uri '/one'
(2) rewrite /one -> /usr/local/apache/htdocs/two.html
(2) local path result: /usr/local/apache/htdocs/two.html
(1) go ahead with /usr/local/apache/htdocs/two.html [OK]
(2) init rewrite engine with requested uri /favicon.ico
(3) applying pattern '^/one' to uri '/favicon.ico'
(1) pass through /favicon.ico
```

Considered in this fashion, it's a lot easier to read.

The initial number indicates the level of the log message. You'll notice that they are all between 1 and 3. Setting RewriteLogLevel to 9 is an old habit and doesn't hurt anything. However, the log messages that you will see will usually be between 1 and 5.

Following the log level is the message itself. For the most part, these are very clear and self-explanatory. So let's follow the conversation as it happened when I requested http://localhost/one:

```
(2) init rewrite engine with requested uri /one
```

init rewrite engine indicates the beginning of a new request. The RewriteEngine On directive has been encountered, and mod_rewrite has received the requested URI and is ready to do something with it. The most important thing to notice at this point is what

Apache thinks the requested URI is. Note that the leading slash is part of the URI. If this rule set had appeared in an `.htaccess` file, that slash would not have been there. This is one of the most common causes of a `RewriteRule` not working the way that you expect it to, and so it's the very first thing you should look at when reading the log file.

```
(3) applying pattern '^/one' to uri '/one'
```

The first `RewriteRule` is applied to the requested URI.

```
(2) rewrite /one -> /usr/local/apache/htdocs/two.html
(2) local path result: /usr/local/apache/htdocs/two.html
```

It matched! The request has been rewritten, and the resulting path is `/usr/local/apache/htdocs/two.html`.

```
(1) go-ahead with /usr/local/apache/htdocs/two.html [OK]
```

The request was fulfilled successfully.

```
(2) init rewrite engine with requested uri /favicon.ico
```

The `init rewrite engine` bit indicates that a new request has started. What's this? I didn't request `/favicon.ico`! But I left this in here because you'll see lots of these in your log files, and it's important to know what they mean, if you don't already.

Most browsers request a file called `/favicon.ico` the first time you go to a website. The resulting image, if found, will be displayed in the address bar of your browser. I imagine you've seen these on various websites. Consequently, you'll see requests for this file all over your log files, regardless of whether or not you have one. And you can reduce the number of gratuitous 404 error messages that appear in your error log by creating such a file. You can obtain more information about `favicon.ico` files and how to create them at http://en.wikipedia.org/wiki/Favicon.

```
(3) applying pattern '^/one' to uri '/favicon.ico'
(1) pass through /favicon.ico
```

mod_rewrite compares the `RewriteRule` to the request for `/favicon.ico`, and since it doesn't match, it simply passes the request through to the rest of the URL mapping phase.

Loop Avoidance

In the second example, a slightly more complex rewrite is used, introducing a `RewriteCond`. This time, I'll omit the `favicon.ico` requests, since they don't really contribute to understanding what's going on.

The example this time uses the following rule set:

```
RewriteEngine On
RewriteCond %{REQUEST_URI} !^/two.html$
RewriteRule ^/two /usr/local/apache/htdocs/two.html
```

The URL being requested this time is http://localhost/two. The transcript from the log looks like the following:

```
(2) init rewrite engine with requested uri /two
(3) applying pattern '^/two' to uri '/two'
(4) RewriteCond: input='/two' pattern='!^/two.html$' => matched
(2) rewrite /two -> /usr/local/apache/htdocs/two.html
(2) local path result: /usr/local/apache/htdocs/two.html
(1) go-ahead with /usr/local/apache/htdocs/two.html [OK]
```

Remember that I have removed the initial part of the log line, for the sake of making this easier to read. Once again, I'll step through the entries, although most of them will look very much like the previous ones.

```
(2) init rewrite engine with requested uri /two
```

As before, the rewrite engine fires up when the request is made, and we can see what mod_rewrite perceives the requested URI to be.

```
(3) applying pattern '^/two' to uri '/two'
```

As before, the requested URI is compared to the pattern in the RewriteRule to see if it should be rewritten.

```
(4) RewriteCond: input='/two' pattern='!^/two.html$' => matched
```

Although the RewriteCond appears before the RewriteRule in the configuration file, it actually isn't checked unless the rule itself already matched. In this case, the value /two is compared to the pattern and found not to match, so we can go ahead with the rewrite.

```
(2) rewrite /two -> /usr/local/apache/htdocs/two.html
(2) local path result: /usr/local/apache/htdocs/two.html
(1) go-ahead with /usr/local/apache/htdocs/two.html [OK]
```

As before, the rewrite is performed, and the resulting target is served successfully.

It is worthwhile to compare these log entries to what happens in two other cases. First, consider the case when we request http://localhost/two.html, which should not be rewritten:

```
(2) init rewrite engine with requested uri /two.html
(3) applying pattern '^/two' to uri '/two.html'
(4) RewriteCond: input='/two.html' pattern='!^/two.html$' => not-matched
(1) pass through /two.html
```

The RewriteRule pattern is compared to the requested URI and matches, but when the RewriteCond fails, the requested URI is passed through unchanged.

And when a URI is requested that doesn't match any of the rules, such as http://localhost/one, we see the following:

```
(2) init rewrite engine with requested uri /one
(3) applying pattern '^/two' to uri '/one'
(1) pass through /one
```

The RewriteRule is compared, found not to match, and the request is passed through unchanged, without the RewriteCond being considered at all.

RewriteRule in .htaccess Files

For the third example, we'll move the rewrite rule to an .htaccess file, to demonstrate the differences when executing a RewriteRule in a per-directory scope. As we discussed very early in the book, when in a per-dir context, everything is assumed to be relative to that directory. Thus, every time a file path is considered, that directory path is removed from the path and then put back on when we're done.

■Note In order for this example to work, you'll need to have RewriteLog turned on in the main server configuration file, since this directive is not permitted in .htaccess files.

For this example, consider the following .htaccess file:

```
RewriteEngine On
RewriteRule ^one two.html
```

Notice that the leading slash has been removed from the RewriteRule pattern. You'll see why as we look through the log file.

This .htaccess file is placed in the root directory of our server, /usr/local/apache/htdocs. The URL http://localhost/one is requested, resulting in the following sequence of log file entries.

```
(3) [per-dir /usr/local/apache/htdocs/] strip per-dir prefix:
/usr/local/apache/htdocs/one -> one
(3) [per-dir /usr/local/apache/htdocs/] applying pattern '^one' to uri 'one'
(2) [per-dir /usr/local/apache/htdocs/] rewrite one -> two.html
(3) [per-dir /usr/local/apache/htdocs/] add per-dir prefix: two.html ->
/usr/local/apache/htdocs/two.html
(2) [per-dir /usr/local/apache/htdocs/] strip document_root prefix:
/usr/local/apache/htdocs/two.html -> /two.html
(1) [per-dir /usr/local/apache/htdocs/] internal redirect with /two.html
[INTERNAL REDIRECT]
(3) [per-dir /usr/local/apache/htdocs/] strip per-dir prefix:
/usr/local/apache/htdocs/two.html -> two.html
(3) [per-dir /usr/local/apache/htdocs/] applying pattern '^one' to uri
'two.html'
 (1) [perdir /usr/local/apache/htdocs/] pass through
/usr/local/apache/htdocs/two.html
```

This sequence is a little longer than when the directives were in the main Apache configuration file, because quite a bit more is going on. As before, we'll step through it one action at a time.

```
(3) [per-dir /usr/local/apache/htdocs/] strip per-dir prefix:
/usr/local/apache/htdocs/one -> one
```

By the time we reach an .htaccess file or a <Directory> scope, the entire URL mapping procedure has already been navigated, and the requested URL has already been mapped into a file system path. Consequently, what we have at this point is a file path, and not a URI at all. Thus, the RewriteRule pattern needs to be applied to a file path, instead of the URI that was originally requested.

The entry from the rewrite log reflects this fact. Instead of seeing the requested URI, which was /one, we see instead the file path to which it was mapped, namely /usr/local/apache/htdocs/one. The first thing that happens, then, is that mod_rewrite recognizes that we are in a per-dir context, and it removes that per-dir prefix from the path, so that what remains can be compared to the RewriteRule pattern.

A consequence of this is that the resulting URI that we're dealing with is one instead of /one, as it would be were we not in per-dir context. This is extremely important to keep in mind, since the difference between per-dir and regular contexts is the source of the majority of mod_rewrite related problems.

```
(3) [per-dir /usr/local/apache/htdocs/] applying pattern '^one' to uri 'one'
```

Now that the directory prefix has been removed, the `RewriteRule` pattern gets applied to what's left. Since it matches, we move on to the next step.

```
(2) [per-dir /usr/local/apache/htdocs/] rewrite one -> two.html
```

The rewrite occurs, and we have `two.html` as the new URI.

```
(3) [per-dir /usr/local/apache/htdocs/] add per-dir prefix: two.html ->
/usr/local/apache/htdocs/two.html
```

Now that we're done rewriting, the per-dir prefix needs to get added back on, so that we have an actual file path that can be sent to the client.

```
(2) [per-dir /usr/local/apache/htdocs/] strip document_root prefix:
/usr/local/apache/htdocs/two.html -> /two.html
(1) [per-dir /usr/local/apache/htdocs/] internal redirect with /two.html
[INTERNAL REDIRECT]
```

At this point, the resulting file path is converted back into a request URI, and that request is sent back to the URL mapping process to figure out what to do with it.

```
(3) [per-dir /usr/local/apache/htdocs/] strip per-dir prefix:
/usr/local/apache/htdocs/two.html -> two.html
(3) [per-dir /usr/local/apache/htdocs/] applying pattern '^one' to uri ➥
'two.html'
(1) [per-dir /usr/local/apache/htdocs/] pass through
/usr/local/apache/htdocs/two.html
```

The process starts all over again with the rewritten URI. This time around, it doesn't match the pattern, and so the request is passed through untouched. It is, however, very easy to get into a situation where the request loops, if you're not careful to eliminate conditions where the target matches the pattern.

Regex Building Tools

As the regular expressions you are working with become gradually more complex, it becomes useful to have a tool that can help you test these expressions and see what they actually mean. With the combination of the `RewriteLog` telling you what mod_rewrite thinks your URI looks like, and a regular expression tool to test your regular expression against that URI, you can solve these problems much more quickly, as well as gaining valuable insight into how regular expressions iterate through a string.

My personal favorite one of these tools is called Rebug, available from `http://real.jall.org:81/perl/rebug/`. Rebug is written in Perl, using the Perl/Tk libraries, so these must be installed before you can use it. Since it is in Perl, it can be used on any platform where Perl is available.

Rebug's simple interface allows you to put in a regular expression and the pattern you wish to test it against, and see whether or not it matches, as well as which parts of the string match. You can also watch particular expressions, such as $1, $2, and so on, to see what values they get assigned.

Figure 12-1 shows the Rebug interface with a hostname regular expression, complete with what $1 was set to when the match was complete.

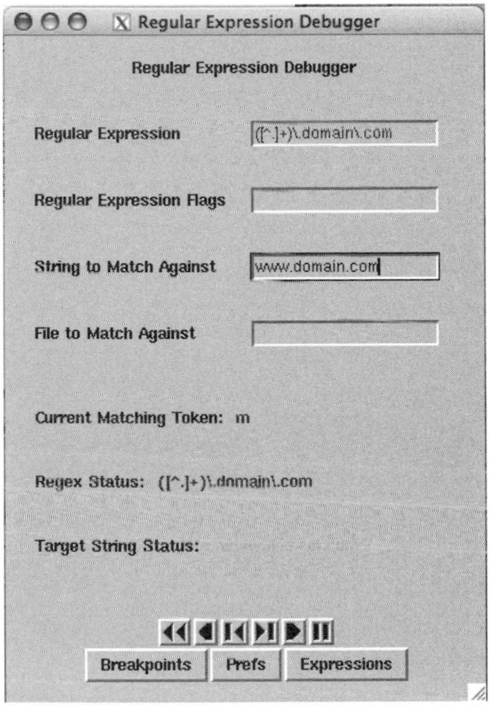

Figure 12-1. *Debugging with Rebug*

Figure 12-2 shows Rebug displaying the value that $1 has been assigned by the end of the matching process.

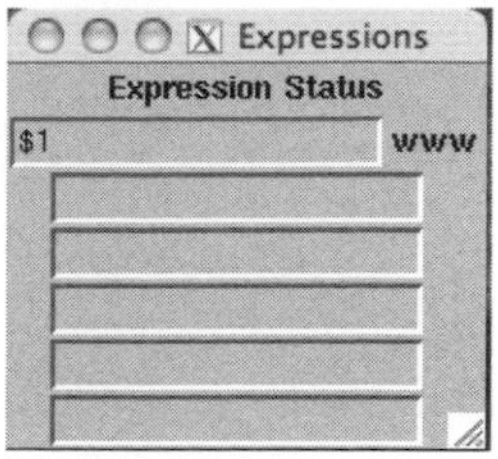

Figure 12-2. *Displaying values assigned during the matching process*

Several other applications of this type exist, one of the best of which is Regex Coach, which you can you obtain from http://www.weitz.de/regex-coach/. A few online tools are also available, which, although they tend to be less full-featured, will usually do the job. One such tool is available at http://www.quanetic.com/regex.php and includes the ability to tell you what the backreferences ($1, $2, etc.) are set to at the end of the match.

For those more attuned to the command line, there is also the pcretest utility, which comes with the pcre library. It allows you to compare a regular expression against a test pattern, telling you what matched and the values of any backreferences, if any.

Summary

The RewriteLog is going to be your most useful tool when attempting to troubleshoot your rewrite rule sets. As you become more familiar with regular expression syntax, the most common cause of confusion in mod_rewrite is the difference between rewrite expressions in the main configuration file versus those in .htaccess files.

Setting up a test server on a machine that you completely control, such as your desktop computer, is an almost essential part of really learning mod_rewrite, since if you're not the server administrator, there's really no way to effectively use the RewriteLog. Once you have your rules working correctly on the test server, you can move them to the production server and be assured that they will work correctly there.

APPENDIX

■■■

Additional Resources

This appendix points out the rather short list of online and other resources available for further assistance with mod_rewrite.

Online Resources

Online resources for mod_rewrite are rather sparse, and many of the online resources contain information that is incorrect or outdated. The following listing presents a few of the better websites where you can find information on mod_rewrite:

- *mod_rewrite Cookbook* (http://rewrite.drbacchus.com/): Initially started as a scratch pad for the book you are now holding, this site is a collection of practical solutions to common problems. It contains many of the recipes in this book, as well as those in the Rewrite Guide in the online documentation.

- *Apache mod_rewrite* (http://httpd.apache.org/docs/2.1/rewrite/): The documentation for mod_rewrite has traditionally been a little intimidating. This is understandable, given the complexity and power of the module. But there is an effort under way, at the time of this writing, to refurbish the documentation and make it friendlier to the beginner.

- *Apache mod_rewrite URL Rewriting Engine* (http://httpd.apache.org/docs/mod/mod_rewrite.html): The official mod_rewrite documentation is the place to go for authoritative information about the module and its configuration options.

Books

Mastering Regular Expressions, Second Edition by Jeffrey Friedl (O'Reilly, 2002), often referred to as just MRE, is the definitive work on regular expressions.

   Regular Expression Recipes: A Problem-Solution Approach by Nathan A. Good (Apress, 2005) presents a compendium of 100 regular expression solutions for PHP, Perl, Python, grep, sed, and Vim.

PCRE Documentation

PCRE stands for *Perl Compatible Regular Expressions.* To understand PCRE, you should turn to Perl. At the command line on any machine with Perl installed, type **perldoc perlre** for the Perl regular expression documentation. Or read it online at `http://perldoc.perl.org/perlre.html`.

Index